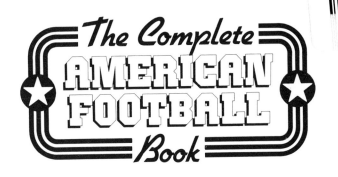

Nicky Horne has been a dedicated fan of American football since seeing his first live game on a visit to the States in 1974. Immediately smitten, he has crammed in as many live and TV games as possible on his many visits since.

In late 1982 he presented the first of Channel Four's American Football programmes which have since become a weekly must for over 5 million viewers.

Well known as a presenter, interviewer and DJ on radio and television, notably with Capital Radio, Nicky has long been an enthusiast for things American, particularly American music.

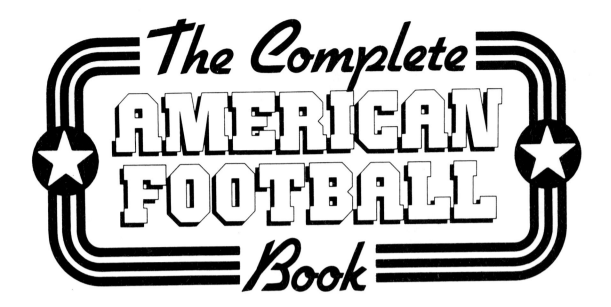

The Complete AMERICAN FOOTBALL Book

NICKY HORNE

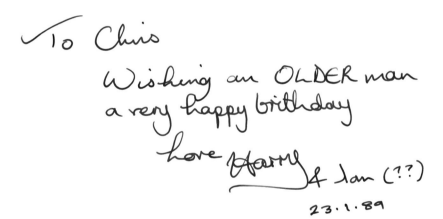

To Chris
Wishing an OLDER man
a very happy birthday
love Harry & Ian (??)
23.1.89

 Robson Books

**Designed by Paul Butters and Harold King,
assisted by Christine Copsey and Pam Mara
Illustrations by Debbie Ryder**

Cover design by David Butler

*Front cover photographs copyright
All-sport; they show* left *26, Mike
Haddix, Eagles v 49ers and* (right)
Eric Dickerson, LA Rams

First published in Great Britain in hardback in 1986
by Robson Books Ltd, Bolsover House, 5–6 Clipstone
Street, London W1P 7EB. This Robson paperback
edition first published in 1987.

Copyright © 1987 Nicky Horne and Robson Books

British Library Cataloguing in Publication Data
Horne, Nicky
    The complete American football book.
    1. Football
    I. Title
    796.332   GV951

    ISBN 0–86051–432–3

Printed in Great Britain by Hazell Watson & Viney,
Aylesbury, Bucks

Bound by Dorstel Press Ltd, Harlow, Essex

CONTENTS

FOREWORD

Like most British people I originally thought that American football was a cissy form of our own rugby game: the padding, the elaborate rest periods, the substitutions, etc. have given rise to this myth on our side of the pond.

Having married an American and consequently made frequent trips to the States, I started to realise that in fact it was a completely different ball game, not at all like rugby and although I am no great expert, my enjoyment increases as I find out more about the sport.

If friends ask me how I go about understanding the game, I explain that the key is to look out for the quarterback (the man in the centre of the field who holds the ball at the beginning of each move). Once you

know that you have to follow him things become relatively simple. He has three options: to make a pass, hand off to a running back, or to run with the ball himself.

It was a great surprise to me to learn that there are effectively three teams on each side: the big guys in defense: the ones whose job it is to gain territory, the offense and the special teams who come on in risky situations.

Armed with these simple facts and many others that will no doubt become clear as you read Nicky's book, you will enjoy the game even more. I have come to appreciate American football: no longer do I think it is a game for cissies!

Paul McCartney

INTRODUCTION

The nearest thing to bedlam is a locker room after a game of American football, especially a play-off. As soon as the teams come off the field they go to their separate rooms and usually within three minutes (the length of a television commercial break in America) the press are allowed in. Players are undressing, throwing their sweat-sodden uniforms into huge bins. Young apprentice equipment managers are cutting the tape off the players' bodies. The noise is deafening as players congratulate their fellow team members on good plays, equipment people shout for pads and helmets; players dive into the showers and emerge clean but battle-weary and all the time the press are there recording the event.

Sometimes there can be as many as twenty camera crews, all with attendant presenters and paraphernalia. Then there are the radio people and press journalists. We all make a bee-line for the men of the match and one player, a giant on the field, is suddenly dwarfed by a horde of cameras, microphones, tape recorders and journalists. We all fight to get a question in . . . it's utter madness.

The first time I went into a locker room, I wasn't ready for all this. I'm not very tall — five foot one — so I couldn't see the player, let alone ask him a question! I discovered that my lack of height was an advantage: by squeezing round the legs of the tv crews I could get to the front. This I did on my first visit to Giants Stadium, the New York Giants' ground in New Jersey. But what happened next took me completely by surprise.

I asked a question: 'Well, you won today, was it as easy as it looked?' The place went quiet . . . I couldn't understand it — the question was a bit naïve, but still . . . Then I realised it was my British voice . . . What is a small bearded 'Limey' doing here?

'American football is now on British television — it's very popular . . .' Then the press turned their attention to me and I was being interviewed!

We also caused a bit of a stir because our camera person was a very attractive young woman and women are not normally seen in this male domain. So that combination of a camerawoman and a British voice made us a curiosity.

Since then things have changed enormously. All the teams are aware of how popular American football is in Britain and no longer are we a curiosity!

I've written this book simply because I felt that there was a need for it. I know there are books on American football, but I wanted something I could give to a fan that would have everything in it, from team histories to football trivia, from superstars to Super Bowls. This is a book I would buy for my son who is fourteen and is mad keen on the game . . . I'd also give it to my fifty-five year old uncle! I have not written this as a technical book — there are some fine books on the technical aspects of the game like *The Illustrated NFL Playbook*.

I hope you enjoy reading this and that you will gain much pleasure from it. I've enjoyed writing it very much and I hope you will learn more about the game that to me is the greatest sporting spectacle on earth.

You'll find information on 16 superstars throughout the book — these are my own selection of players I rate highly. Your favourite may not be included — you can't please everybody but I hope you enjoy reading my choice.

Acknowledgements

To Nick Halling and Debra Shipley without whom . . .

. . . and not forgetting *Gridiron* magazine . . .

My thanks to all the NFL teams. To the NFL in New York for all their help and guidance. I would not have been able to complete this without information from the Official NFL Records Fact Book and the Official NFL Encyclopaedia of Pro Football. At my publishers, for help beyond the call of duty, thanks to Cheryll Roberts, Valerie Passmore and Nancy Duin. Thanks also to my agent Garry Wicks and to Mike Roberts. And very special thanks to my old chum Paul McCartney for sparing the time in a hectic schedule to write such a smashing foreword . . . Good on yer, Paul!

Nicky Horne
June 1987

It's All In A State of Mind

If you think you are beaten, you are;
If you think you dare not, you won't;
If you like to win, but don't think you can,
It's almost a cinch you won't.

If you think you'll lose, you're lost;
For out in the world you'll find,
Success begins with a fellow's will;
It's all in a state of mind.

For many a game is lost
'Ere even a play is run,
And many a coward fails
'Ere even his work is begun.

Think big and your deeds will grow,
Think small and you'll fall behind;
Think that you can and you will;
It's all in a state of mind.

If you think you're out-classed, you are;
You've got to think high to rise;
You've got to be sure of yourself before
You can ever win a prize.

Life's battles don't always go
To the faster or stronger man,
But sooner, or later, the man who wins
Is the fellow who thinks he can.

Walter D. Wintle.

HISTORY

The birth of a game

Let us give praise to William Webb Ellis, the father of rugby and the grandfather of American football.

In November 1816 a new boy arrived at Rugby public school; born in Ireland he was the son of James Ellis, a soldier who had died a few years before. His mother, who had family in Rugby, took advantage of Rugby school being free to the sons of residents of the City, and accordingly William Webb Ellis became a day boy.

He was very successful in his academic career, reaching the sixth form at the early age of 15. Not only did he excel in his academic work, but he was also showing his prowess on the cricket pitch where he was an excellent and gifted all-rounder. All in all William Webb Ellis was the perfect schoolboy.

Although cricket was the main official sport played at Rugby the boys used to organise their own games in the playground purely for fun. There were conventions, rather than rules, and they changed with every game depending on how many boys were there and how they felt at the time. One of these games was a primitive version of soccer. One convention even in this most disorganised game was that no-one was allowed to pick up the ball and run with it — it was permitted to knock the ball in flight with the arm or the fist but that was all. Ellis was not a rule breaker — then at least, and joined in these free-for-alls during the breaks and after school.

It was when he entered the sixth form that Ellis was to break the rules. It's interesting that by this time he had chosen his career — he wanted to be a vicar — in those days a 'cushy little number' for boys of his class and intellect. One would not imagine a boy with such high aspirations ever daring to break with convention — but break he did and in doing so fathered not one, but two, national sports.

Despite what you may have read elsewhere, no-one is absolutely sure exactly when it happened: some say November 1823, some November 1825. The reason for the confusion is that at the time what Ellis did was not seen as momentous and it was only written about some considerable time later — what is certain is that the event took place in the autumn of 1823, 4 or 5.

The man who first picked up the ball and ran with it — William Webb Ellis in later years as the vicar of St Clement Danes

Rugby School in the nineteenth century — where and when it all began

The event was quite simply that during one of these disorganised games, after a long and scoreless game, the ball was kicked high into the air and Ellis caught it in his arms. According to the rules he ought to have retired as far as he liked, without parting with the ball, for the opposite side could advance only as far as the spot where he had caught the ball, and were unable to rush forward till he had either punted it, or had placed it for someone else to kick — it was by means of these placed kicks that most of the goals were scored. Ellis disregarded the rule, and instead of retiring backwards rushed forward with the ball in his hands towards the opposite goal and rugby was born.

English emigrants then took the games of rugby and soccer to America, and although no definite proof exists there is a strong possibility that Thomas Hughes, the author of *Tom Brown's Schooldays* which was about Rugby school, took the game, and possibly an oval ball, to America when he went there on a speaking tour of colleges when his book was published.

Early days in America

The formal beginning of American football is usually seen as the match between Rutgers and Princeton colleges on 6 November 1869 (Rutgers won 6–4). During the 1880s English Rugby Union rules gave way to a distinctively American college sport, particularly under Walter Camp of Yale University, who is hailed as the 'father of American football'. He replaced the rugby scrum with the line of scrimmage and was instrumental in cutting the number of players from rugby's 15 to American football's 11.

The rules have changed enormously since then, in major and minor elements of the game. One of the most far-reaching was the 1906 legalising of the forward pass, forbidden in rugby and early American football. The quarterback had arrived!

Over the years the scoring system has changed

eight times, the size of the field sixteen times and the ball's size eight times.

To get an idea of what early college football was like here is an extract from the Rugby School magazine of 1890 which describes marvellously how a rugby player saw this fascinating sport.

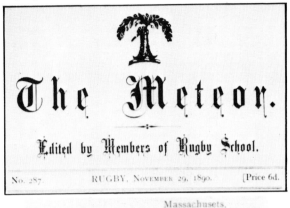

The Meteor.

Edited by Members of Rugby School.

No. 287.   RUGBY, NOVEMBER 29, 1890.   [Price 6d.

Massachusets, Institute of Technology.

I went out the other day to see what the Americans call Football, and was not much edified. They never touch the ball with their feet the whole game through (except for a place kick), and when the ball is dead, instead of having a good old scrummage, they form up in line, and one man has his hand on the ball; he kind of 'fotckes' it back with his hand to the half-back who is standing behind him, and then charges the opposing line to prevent them tackling the three-quarters. I hope the enclosed cutting will make it clearer. It is a tremendously scientific game as you will see, and everything is worked by a secret code of numbers, so you hear the captains calling out in this manner, 17, 14, 11; 46, 32; 19, 26; 30, 7, 31; and I suppose every number means some movement. It is, however, extremely rough, and eight out of the eleven men have been known to be hurt at it, while almost every game sees somebody laid out; so much is this so, that five substitutes are allowed by law, and very often this number is required. I have not attempted to play it, and do not intend to, for though I do not mind a few knocks, still I do not want to break a limb, or to engage in a game where hitting with fists is freely indulged in. There is, however, a feeling I think, growing up for a more gentlemanly game, and I hope in a few years the laws will be stricter, and better carried out. Another thing which strikes one here are the college yells, as they are called. Every college has its own, and uses it to cheer its men on with, and in place of the cheer. Ours, for instance, is Em, Eye, Tee. Rah! Rah! Rah! M-I-T. Rah! Rah! Rah! M-I-T. Rah! Rah! Rah! Technology. The first lot being pronounced very sharp and quick, and the Technology coming out with a roar. The John Hopkins University has Hullabaloo, Cannuck, Cannuck Hullabaloo, Cannuck, Cannuck, *Hoo-rah! Hoo-*rah, J-H-U. Harvard's is seven rahs, winding up with Harvard.

Walter Camp, the father of American football. Under him at Yale such distinctive features of American football as downs and yards-to-gain systems and the team of eleven developed.

The following is the "cutting" mentioned, which we will also print *verbatim*, but we are not to be held responsible for the Americanisms thereof—not even for the "tumbling and erratic spheroid."

As football becomes better understood by people outside of the colleges, the popularity of the game increases. Last year it was estimated that from 20,000 to 25,000 people thronged the Berkley Oval to see Yale and Princeton struggle in the mud, and it is probable that these figures will be duplicated at the Yale-Harvard game at Springfield this year and at the Yale-Princeton game in New York.

A popular idea has been that football is a rough, brutal sport where slugging is one of the leading elements, and where blood and broken limbs are the necessary results. At the best, it has been considered by some to be a fierce, hard struggle of endurance, where sheer brute strength was pitted against brute strength, with little reference to the ball, and that victory came when one side was overpowered by the superior strength of the other.

Such an idea does not reach the first principles of the game. To be sure, in a hard fought contest at the end of a season, the contestants receive shocks and falls, any one of which would kill the sympathizing spectator who does nothing more laborious than sign checks and hold a pair of opera-glasses at the theatre. But it should be borne in mind than these young athletes have been toughened by two months of hard and faithful training, till their bodies are practically envelopes of india-rubber. These falls that cause the hearts of mothers and sweethearts to throb so violently, are nothing more than the young gladiators have been sustaining day in and day out for weeks. Occasionally, a sprained ankle, or even a broken limb, may lay a fellow up for a while; but the vigorous, sturdy manhood which is built up by the game, much more than makes up for an occasional season of enforced idleness while the player nurses a swollen limb.

So far from football being a slugging game, it is a fact well known to all players, that the regulation slugger is a poor football player. In the first place, the rule is strict, and the first blow struck in the sight of the umpire sends the player so offending off the field. Granting that some little slugging may be indulged in unseen by the umpire, the fact is fully understood that the man who is watching for a chance to hit his opponent does not keep his eye on the ball, and good captains, in selecting their teams, invariably give the fighting player the go-by. Moreover, brute strength will come very far from winning games. How often has the football player seen an eleven of giants, say from the University of Michigan, pitted against an occasional lightweight team from Yale, Harvard or Princeton, with the same invariable result. The big, untrained men are not in it compared with their lighter but better-trained opponents, and they are invariably snowed under a big score.

The game of football, as now played by the colleges, requires a combination of qualities, chief among which is unison of movement, or team work. The successful captain needs to possess all the qualities of a great general. He must have studied the game deeply, and mastered all the moves of preceding successful teams. More than this, he must be an inventor. After days of thought, he evolves some way of making one man do the work for which his opponents require two—he plots out some new and better way of carrying out some well-worn trick, and the result is shown in a deciding touchdown or goal made at a critical point of the final game for the championship.

To make up a successful team the members must be quick, active and strong, with endurance practically limitless. Fast running, expert dodging, sure catching of the tumbling, erratic spheroid in the face of a hostile mob, strong and accurate kicking, absolute fearlessness of personal injury, and a sturdy resolution to fight for victory till the last gasp—all these are the abilities and qualities which find perpetual expression upon the football field.

As the uninitiated sees a score of human beings squirming and wriggling over a "down" he does not understand that every one of those 22 players had a well defined duty to perform, and when the coveted five yards is not gained, the captain can point with certainty to the man who failed to carry out his part of the programme. Every movement of the many which seem so purposeless has been planned out and executed dozens of times before.

A few of the simplest moves may be here explained as illustrating the way in which the game is played. At the beginning of the game, from the kick-off, the wedge or V trick, is usually tried. This consists of forming the players into a wedge, with one man in the centre having the ball. Shoulder to shoulder, the members of the team charge the opposing line, and if they succeed in getting by the other rush-line, the man with the ball slips out of the wedge and runs down the field, still more or less protected by his associates.

Another method of gaining ground is by the quarter-back passing the ball to a half-back, who is then driven through a "hole" in the opposing rush line. These holes are made by the rushers in a place designated by the signal, which is understood by all the team.

A third method of gaining ground is around the end. In this trick the ball is passed to a half-back who runs around one end of his rush-line. The rushers on that side of the line force their opponents inward. If the move is successful and the runner gets around the end without being tackled, he must then get past the opposing half-backs and full-backs, to do which he is assisted by his three associate backs, who run ahead of him and "block off" or ward off his opponents by bumping into them.

When these moves are well executed they look very pretty, but when one of the opponents gets free and tackles and throws the runner, the move is frustrated. In blocking off, or interfering, the arms cannot be used, and to hold with the arms an opponent who has not the ball is a foul.

A fourth method of ground gaining is by kicking the ball. If the side having the ball does not advance it five yards or lose 20 yards in three downs, the ball is given to the opponents. So, on the third down the ball is usually passed back to the full back, who kicks or "punts" the ball far down the field.

These four methods in general represent the way the ball is advanced. To prevent aimless shoving the man with the ball can at any time call "down" or any opponent who has tackled the man and hold the ball can call "held," in which case the ball must be put down for a scrummage. The rushers line up opposite one another and the centre rush rolls or "snaps" the ball back to the quarter-back who passes it to some third player for a run similar to those already described.

As a matter of fact, every player in the eleven

takes some part in every play. When one half-back runs with the ball, the other three backs run with and ahead of him, and block off opponents so that they cannot tackle the runner. The "holes" in the rush-line are made at any point when the weakness of individual men, or their improper alignment, seem to offer the best opening. For every one of the 30 or 40 moves which each eleven can make there is a definite signal, given usually by the quarter-back and understood by every member of the team. When the signal is given every man knows what is expected of him, and the instant the ball is snapped back, every man begins to do his allotted work.

The score is made by safeties, touchdowns and goals. A safety is made when a side, by its own volition or misplay, touches the ball down in its own goal, and counts two for the opponents. A touchdown is made when a player carries the ball across the opponents' goal-line, and there touches it down. A goal from touchdown is made by the ball being kicked over the goal bar from a place where it is held on the ground by one of the side which scored the touchdown. If the try-at-goal be successful, it adds two points to the four scored by the touchdown. A goal from the field is scored by a "drop-kick," which sends the ball over the bar, and counts five points.

In the late nineteenth and early twentieth centuries football grew and increased in popularity but the degree of violence involved was horrendous — so savage was the game that in 1905, 18 college players died and 159 were seriously injured. The outcry went all the way to the Oval office where President Roosevelt ordered 'This must stop, or I'll see that football is ended.' Roosevelt summoned the college leaders to the White House and new rules were drafted to help prevent injury.

Pro football's story

In 1920 Jim Thorpe was named president of the American Professional Football Association (APFA), newly formed at Canton, Ohio. Thorpe, an ex-college player who had represented his country in the 1912 Olympic games, recalled some time later: 'A bunch of men paid $100 each for a franchise, and in no time at all most of us were broke'. The APFA was re-organised in 1922 as the 18-team National Football League (NFL).

Jim Thorpe, first president of the American Professional Football Association, founded in 1920, and voted the top American athlete of the first half of the twentieth century

William (Pudge) Heffelfinger, the first football player in America to be paid for his services, making him in 1892 the earliest professional football player

In 1923 the NFL had 20 teams, in order of 1923 standings:

Canton Bulldogs
Chicago Bears
Green Bay Packers
Milwaukee Badgers
Cleveland Indians
Chicago Cardinals
Duluth Kelleys
Buffalo All-Americans
Columbus Tigers
Racine Legion

Toledo Maroons
Rock Island Independents
Minneapolis Marines
St Louis All-Stars
Hammond Pros
Dayton Triangles
Akron Indians
Oorang Indians
Rochester Jeffersons
Louisville Brecks

The Chicago Staleys under the guidance of the legendary George Halas became the Chicago Bears: and it was in 1925 that pro football began to emerge as a real force when Halas persuaded the nationally idolised Red Grange — the 'galloping ghost' — to turn professional. The crowds flocked to see the Bears and Grange and the NFC was on its way.

In 1926 Red Grange's manager, the aptly named C.C. (Cash & Carry) Pyle, told the Chicago Bears that unless the 'galloping ghost' became a very rich poltergeist (a five-figure sum was the starting point) he would pull Grange out of the Chicago Bears. Pyle was a very smooth operator and knew that the Bears would refuse to pay such an exorbitant sum — but he had other ideas. He wanted to start his own league with Grange as the central figure, and when the

Bears refused to pay up Pyle leased Yankee Stadium in New York and started his own league. He called it the American Football League. Red Grange played for Pyle's team — the New York Yankees. The other AFL teams were:

Boston Bulldogs
Brooklyn Horsemen
Chicago Bulls
Cleveland Panthers

Newark Bears
Philadelphia Quakers
Los Angeles Wildcats
Rock Island Independents

We've all seen the wave, that co-ordinated rise and fall of the hands around a stadium. They were even doing it at the World Cup. Where did it originate? It was in the mid sixties in Washington, when the college team the Huskys was suffering a losing streak, its 'rooting' section had their lettered cards taken away from them because of rowdiness. With nothing to hold they needed something to do with their hands. So Rob Waller, the head cheerleader invented the wave. It was then taken to pro football by 'Bill the Beer Man', who was a vendor at the Husky stadium and at the Kingdome, Seattle. He introduced it to Seattle fans and after a few appearances on tv — it caught on like wildfire!

In a famous divorce case in New York a separating couple agreed over the division of property and finances, but not on who got the New York Giants' season tickets. The issue went to court and it was ruled that they should go to alternate home games.

A great early team, the 1920 Staley team, forerunner of the Chicago Bears

The league was a flop and folded after one season — but it did make the NFL expand to 22 teams. The times were a-changing! However, professional football suffered a severe depression in the ensuing years and by 1931 there were only 10 teams playing:

> *Brooklyn Dodgers*
> *Chicago Bears*
> *Chicago Cardinals*
> *Cleveland Indians*
> *Frankford Yellowjackets*
> *Green Bay Packers*
> *New York Giants*
> *Portsmouth Spartans*
> *Providence Steamrollers*
> *Stapleton Stapes*

A year later the Steamrollers, the Yellow-jackets, and the Indians had gone — only one team replaced them (the Boston Braves) and so in 1932 the NFL had a mere eight teams.

Things started to improve in 1933. The NFL now had 10 teams and they were divided into two five-team divisions — the winners of each to meet in a championship game at the end of the season. 1933 thus was the birthday of divisions in the NFL and of the championship game.

GEORGE S. HALAS
1895-1983

...pure and simple, he loved this game. He chased it without design, without notion of the fame and wealth it would lead him to. And even when those gifts became reality, the attraction remained the same, always the game. He loved this game...

...a game that was as uncluttered and uncompromising as he was. Its requirements were courage, endurance, self-discipline and a passionate competitiveness. As a young man and all through his life those were his prerequisites, too...

...football, purged of all the adornments, is a very simple game. It is played by men who stand toe-to-toe, look one another in the eye and say, "All right, now let's see which of us is the better man." That concept drew him to the game...

...his "real" monument is the fierce, joyous love he had for the game. And that love was always there. All of the achievements didn't matter as much to him as his love for the game and the joy of competing...

Without him . . . the legendary George Halas, player, founder, owner, coach and much more during half a century of football history

The 'galloping ghost' Red Grange, whose footballing talents drew the first large pro football crowds in the 1920s

With the game becoming more exciting to watch — the forward pass was encouraged, the fans started to increase and by the start of the Second World War league attendance set a new record — over a million Americans had been to see professional football. In 1959 the American Football League was formed by Lamar Hunt and they immediately signed a contract with ABC Television to have their games televised (incidentally it was at this time that players' names were put on the back of their play-shirts) and its eight teams were split into two divisions.

The AFL had to accept second class status for some time, until 1969 when a gifted quarterback, Joe Namath of the New York Jets, vowed that the Jets from the AFL would beat the Baltimore Colts in Super Bowl III. They did 16–7 and in doing so the AFL was granted national recognition.

In 1966 the American Football League merged with the National and it was then that with an expanded NFL the two conferences were formed. The National Football Conference and the American Football Conference were each divided into three — Eastern, Central and Western divisions. In theory geography was the key to which team was placed in what division, but it didn't work out that way — which is why Dallas appears in the NFC East when it's in South Texas, and Atlanta and New Orleans are in the Western division. The conferences are broken up like this:

American Conference Central

Pittsburgh Steelers
Houston Oilers
Cincinnati Bengals
Cleveland Browns

American Conference East

Buffalo Bills
Baltimore Colts
Miami Dolphins
New England Patriots
New York Jets

National Conference West

Atlanta Falcons
Los Angeles Rams
New Orleans Saints
San Francisco 49ers

National Conference Central

Detroit Lions
Tampa Bay Buccaneers
Green Bay Packers
Chicago Bears
Minnesota Vikings

American Conference West

San Diego Chargers
Denver Broncos
Los Angeles Raiders
Kansas City Chiefs
Seattle Seahawks

National Conference East

Philadelphia Eagles
Dallas Cowboys
St Louis Cardinals
New York Giants
Washington Redskins

Lamar Hunt, who dared challenge the mighty NFL by setting up the American Football League in 1959, was instrumental in the rivals leagues' merger in 1966 . . . and is credited with naming the Super Bowl

Teams that have come and gone

Chicago Cardinals
Buffalo All-Americans
Akron Pros
Canton Bulldogs
Dayton Triangles
Rock Island Independents
Cleveland Indians

Rochester Jeffersons
Detroit Heralds
Columbus Panhandles
Cincinnati Celts
Portsmouth Spartans
Providence Steamrollers

Stapleton Stapes
Cleveland Indians
Brooklyn Dodgers
Frankford Yellowjackets
Cleveland Rams
New York Yanks
Dallas Texans
Newark Tornadoes

Boston Braves
Cincinnati Reds
St Louis Gunners
Boston Shamrocks
Brooklyn Tigers

Pittsburgh Americans
Rochester Tigers
Los Angeles Bulldogs
Columbus Bullies
Buffalo Americans
Milwaukee Chiefs
Buffalo Tigers
Buffalo Bisons
Chicago Rockets
Los Angeles Dons
Miami Seahawks
Chicago Hornes
Boston Patriots
Chicago Staleys

Yale's 1879 football team, which played in the first 11-man game

FOOTBALL & TELEVISION

TV and football were married on 22 October 1939 on a wet afternoon in New York. There were not many 'guests', with fewer than 1,000 people then owning televisions. But that blurred picture of the Philadelphia Eagles against the Brooklyn Dodgers live from Ebberts Field shown on W2XBS was the start of what has become the perfect marriage between television and sport.

The dollars started flying in the sixties when the tv companies anxious to show the game started bidding against each other in the time-honoured way. In 1964 CBS paid $14.1 million a year for regular occasion rights for two years. *Monday Night Football* broadcast by ABC began in 1970 and a year later Super Bowl VI with nearly 24 million viewers became the only sporting event in history to attract so many fans.

In 1973 the audience for Super Bowl VII had increased to 75 million and this is when the NFL introduced the now familiar numbering system for players.

It wasn't until the 1976 Super Bowl X game between Pittsburgh and Dallas that CBS could claim that the audience of 80 million was the largest for any American tv show of any description. Of course this made a rod for the tv companies' own backs although they could make millions from the advertising. In 1977 in the largest single tv package ever negotiated ABC, CBS, and NBC paid $640 million dollars for the rights to four years' football — regular, post-season and Pro Bowl.

It's easy to overdose on football on tv — every year 800 hours of pro football are televised and there are college games as well. It's possible to spend all weekend watching football on television.

During the 1985 season over 75 million people watched at least one NFL game every week. Super Bowl XX in January 1986 was watched by 127 million, the largest-ever audience for an American tv broadcast. Of the ten largest American audiences ever, eight have been for Super Bowl games and of the six broadcasts ever to have had over 100 million viewers, five were Super Bowl games.

Football's Loss . . .

Actor Burt Reynolds was known as 'Buddy' during his college football days when he posted some impressive statistics for the 1954 Florida State University freshman team; he carried the ball 16 times for 134 yards, an average of 8.4 yards per carry, and scored two touchdowns. That's not all: he also had four receptions for 76 yards and intercepted a pass. He went on to earn varsity letters in 1955 and 1957 — and of course became a film star!

In one regular season game a kick-off was actually replayed because the tv crew wasn't ready and had missed televising it!

What is it about football which makes players want to become American President? The fortieth President, Ronald Reagan, is no exception. But since playing, way back in the 1920s and 30s for Illinois School and Eureka College, he has of course had a number of careers — broadcaster, film actor, tv show host, Governor of California. . .

THE BASICS

If you are not familiar with the basics of the game, this chapter is for you! If you want to go further than I could possibly do in one chapter I strongly recommend you buy an excellent publication called *The Illustrated NFL Playbook*.

The field

Football is played on a field 100 yards long and 160 feet wide. Each end of the field has a ten-yard section beyond, called the end zone, and that is the ultimate goal of each team — to advance to the end zone and score a touchdown. At the back of the end zone are the goal posts which are 18½ feet wide with the cross bar 10 feet above the ground — the goal posts are 20 feet high. The field is sectioned by white lines every 5 yards.

The arrows point towards the nearer goal, the figures are the number of yards to it

Game officials travel more than 125,000 miles per year on 20 weekends. They enforce some 1,800 regulations from a 210-page rule book.

Officials are known as seven blind mice by fans who boo them.

In 1980 visiting pro teams won 45% of games played. In 1981 it dropped to 37.7%. Leaving home is obviously bad for the health.

The Field

Hashmarks
A yard apart and 70 feet 9 inches in from each sideline, they guide the officials in placing the ball before play

Field numbers
Indicate ten-yard distances from the nearer goal line

Yard lines
Divide the field eve[r] five yards

End line
Bounds the shorter sides of the pitch ten yards behind the goal line. The goal posts are in the centre of the end lines

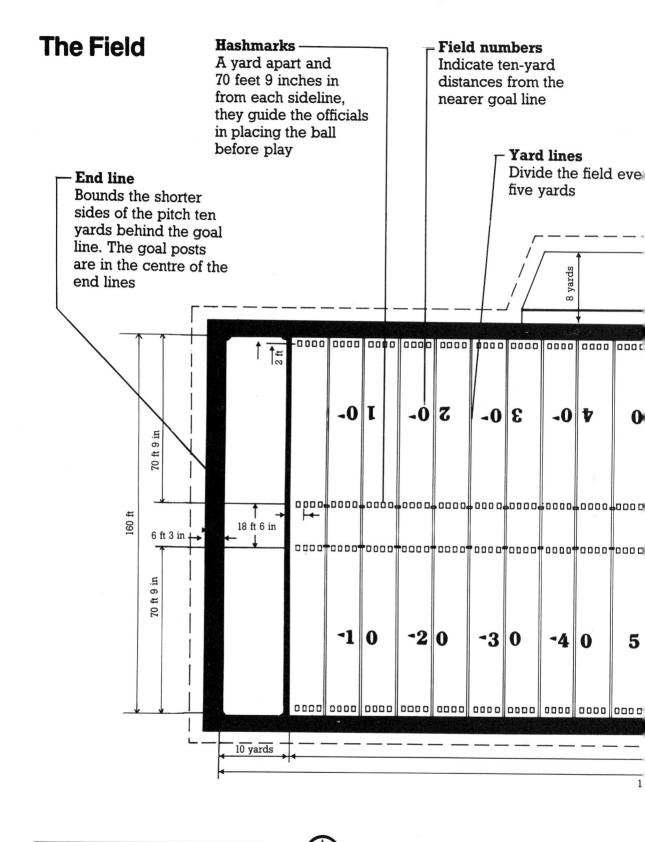

Team benches
For members of the
squad other than the
maximum of 11
allowed on the field at
any one time. They
must be at least ten
yards from the
sidelines

Sidelines
Bound the limit of the
playing area on the
longer sides of the
pitch

Restraining line
A yellow line marking
the limit, six feet
outside the field
border, beyond which
anyone not playing
may not advance

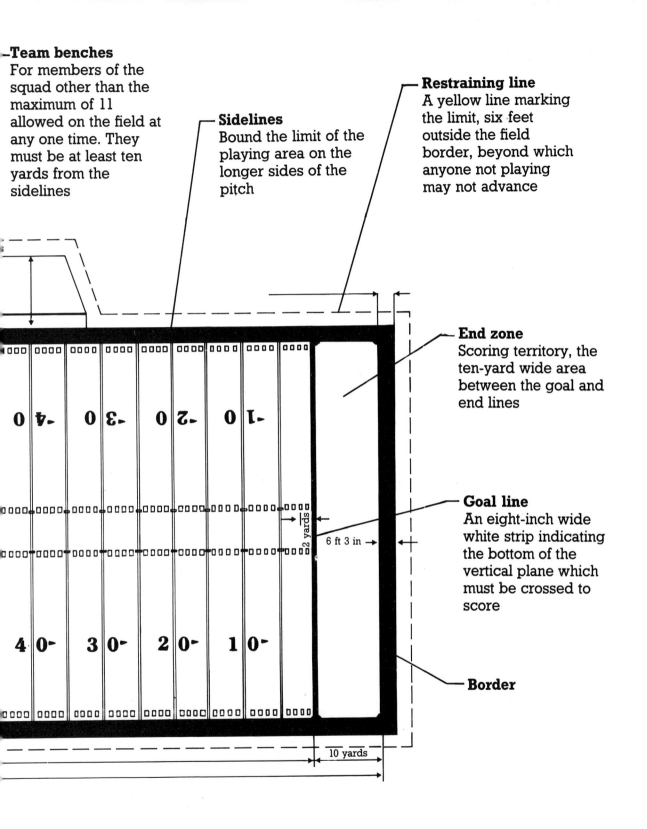

End zone
Scoring territory, the
ten-yard wide area
between the goal and
end lines

Goal line
An eight-inch wide
white strip indicating
the bottom of the
vertical plane which
must be crossed to
score

Border

2 yards

6 ft 3 in →

10 yards

Defensive end Howie Long of the Los Angeles Raiders, about to pounce

The players

Each club has 45 players split into three different teams — the offense, the defense and the special team. The offense's job is to move the ball upfield into the opponent's territory and the defense's job is to stop them. Special teams come on to the field in kicking situations. Only 11 players from each team are allowed on the field at any one time.

Let's look at a typical line-up of offense against defense and give you an idea of who does what.

Offense

Seven of the 11 offensive players must be on 'the line' and these powerful linemen have the job of protecting the other players on the offense, especially the quarterback. Blocking is their art — they block the defense who are doing their hardest to get the ball carrier. An offensive player can block using any part of his body except his hands.

The centre

He's in the middle of the offensive line and it is he who must snap the ball to the quarterback, starting play — once he's done that he stands up and blocks the defense from getting to the quarterback.

Left and right guards

Left and right tackles

These four players are tough and their job is not easy — they open up holes for running players and block the defense on a passing play.

A perfect example of the wide receiver's task

Offense

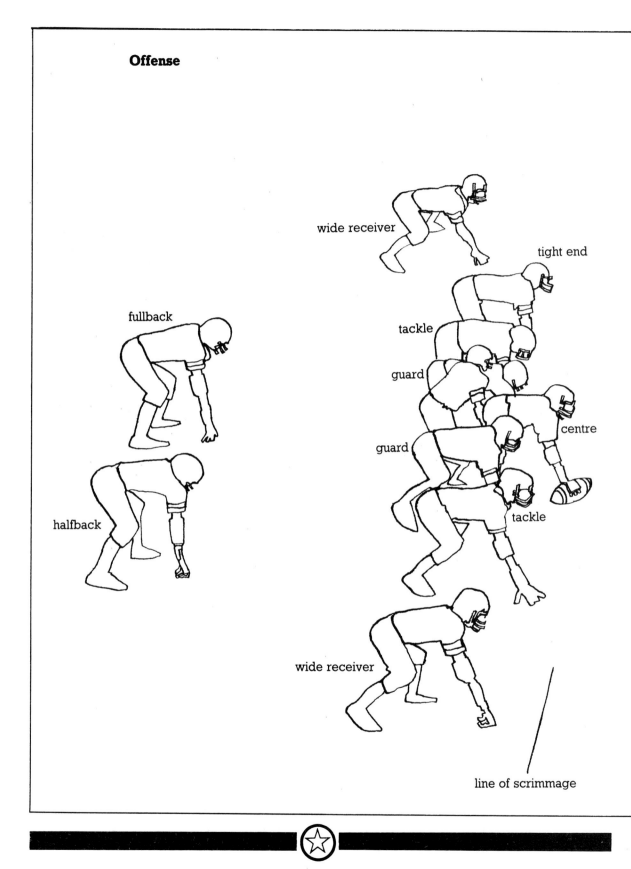

wide receiver

tight end

fullback

tackle

guard

guard

centre

halfback

tackle

wide receiver

line of scrimmage

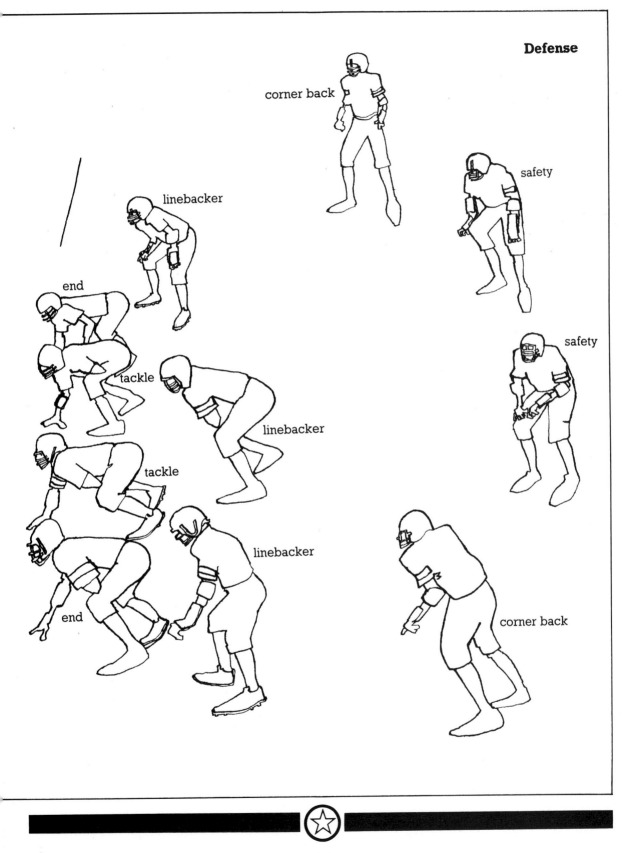

Defense

corner back

safety

safety

linebacker

end

tackle

linebacker

tackle

linebacker

end

corner back

33

Tight end

Versatile and big — that's what tight ends are. They can run with the ball, block the defense, and catch a pass.

Wide receiver

He doesn't need to be big, but he does need to be fast — he's the one who sprints down the field to bag the long bombs.

Halfback or running back

He receives, runs and blocks.

Fullback or running back

This guy needs to be a powerful runner. Normally used when the team needs short yardage.

Quarterback

The field general — he calls the plays, throws the ball, hands it off to his running back or sometimes runs with the ball.

The defense

Left and right tackles and the left and right end. It is with these four front-line men that you have the bulk and strength of a team. These guys are the heavyweights — around 18 to 25 stone.

Linebackers

These are the second line of defense. These guys try to stop running plays, upset or intercept pass plays and sometimes are assigned to attack the quarterback.

Fullback Earnest Byner of the Cleveland Browns breaking a tackle

The shortest pass on record is just 2 inches — the touchdown pass made in 1960 between Eddie La Baron and Dick Bielski.

Corner safeties and safeties

Also known as defensive backs they are 'the secondary'. Their job is varied — on a passing play they must intercept the receiver and foil a long pass and they must also be able to tackle an offensive ball carrier.

The play — the downs systems

How does a team move upfield?

Each offensive team has four attempts to move the ball at least 10 yards — these attempts are known as downs. If they don't make the required 10 yards the other team gets possession. If they do make 10 or more yards they get another four attempts and so on.

Let's give an example:

On their first attempt the offensive moves the ball 2 yards (remember their target is 10). Their next attempt is called second and 8 — that means it's their second go and they are trying to achieve 8 yards or more. Say they make only 6 yards on their second attempt (second down) — it's then called third and 2 — 2 or more yards is their target and it's their third of four attempts.

On the third down they don't make any yardage at all — on their fourth and final down if they are not within field goal range (50 yards-ish) they punt the ball to the other side. That means a specialist kicker comes on and kicks the ball as far into opposition territory as possible. Possession of the ball then changes sides.

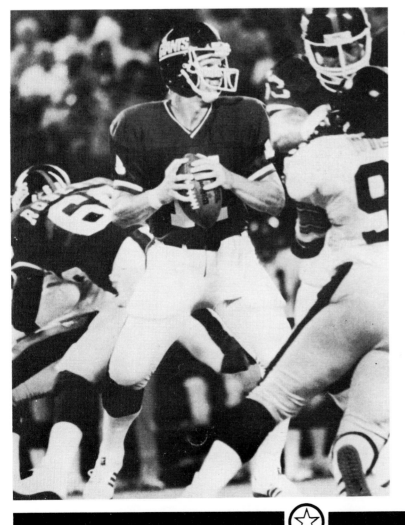

Quarterback Phil Simms of the New York Giants about to throw a long bomb

A rubber band, moved from finger to finger, is used by some referees as a way of keeping track of downs.

Scoring

Touchdown 6 points

Here an offensive player has to be in possession of the ball in the end zone. He doesn't have to touch it down literally as in rugby — just 'break the plane of the goal' — that's an imaginary wall from the goal line all the way up to heaven!

PAT — point after touchdown 1 point

By kicking the ball through the goal posts from the 2-yard line a team 'converts' a touchdown and scores an extra point.

Field goal 3 points

Once again this is scored by kicking the ball through the goal posts, normally no more than 50 yards from the goal line.

Safety 2 points

This is a huge psychological boost and occurs when an offensive ball carrier is tackled in his own end zone.

Playing time

Every game is divided into four 15-minute sections or quarters; after the first two quarters the teams get a half-time breather. So why does a game last more than an hour? Well, there are many ways a team can stop the clock, so an average game lasts a couple of hours at least.

There is also a 30-second clock which starts when the referee blows his whistle and in that time the offense must begin to play.

Conferences, the season, getting to Super Bowl

There are two conferences in the National Football League, the American Conference and the National Conference. Each has 14 teams in three four- or five-team divisions: the Eastern, Central and Western Divisions (see pages 62–3 for team names and locations).

During the late summer/early autumn pre-season rookies are tested and team squads cut to 45. Winning the annual Super Bowl is the

Left: **Rich Karlis of the Denver Broncos scoring a field goal demonstrates the kicker's role**

Right: **Touchdown! The ball has broken the plane of the goal line and the zebra signals a touchdown for six points**

An average passing down takes 5–10 seconds.

The average running play takes 5–7 seconds.

ultimate aim of NFL teams and games which count towards the Super Bowl begin in the autumn. During the September to Christmas main season every team plays 16 games, including one home and one away game against the other three or four teams in the same division. Other games are mainly against other teams in the same conference, although there are some inter-conference games.

A team's main season record is given in a two- or three-figures series (e.g. 9–7, 8–6–2); the first figure is the number of wins, the second the number of losses and a third indicates any ties.

The team with the most wins becomes division champion. Where more than one team has the same number of wins, an elaborate tie-breaking procedure based on other achievements within games determines the championship.

The divisional champions qualify for the post-season play-offs and the two teams in each conference with the next best records qualify as wild card teams.

Between Christmas and late January the divisional winners and wild card teams in each conference play off in the following sequence, and the AFC and NFC champions meet in the Super Bowl at the end of January.

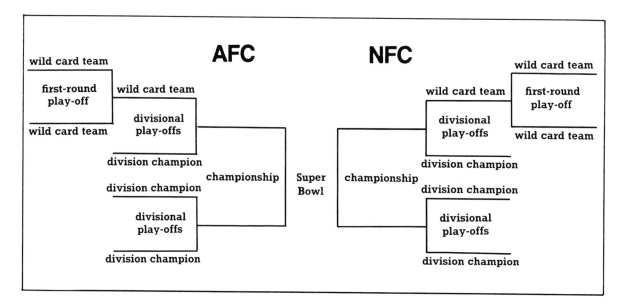

Coach nicknames: Peppy, Buck, Curly, Bo, Pop, Gloomy, Buddy, Lone Star, Jock are reasonable enough, but how about being called Bum! That's the fate of ex-New Orleans coach O.A. Phillips. He got the name as a child from his younger sister's efforts to say 'brother'.

Some Dos and Don'ts

When the player with the ball touches the ground with any part of his body except his feet and hands the ball is 'dead' — no longer legally in play.

Players cannot move the ball forward by hitting it with the hand except to deflect a pass.

A player can pass the ball backwards at any time — but only one forward pass is allowed on each play.

Players cannot trip, kick, knee or punch. They cannot hit a member of the opposition below the shoulder with forearm or elbow; grab the face mask; fall on a player when the ball is dead; block from behind; tackle a player who is out of bounds.

For any of these a team may be penalised by loss of yardage — have a down taken away or worst of all have a player disqualified.

Games are 60 minutes — but it's by no means all action. Taking account of interruptions the ball is actually 'live' for 12–15 minutes out of the prescribed 60.

New York Giants' linebacker Lawrence Taylor attacking a rival quarterback

Eric Dickerson
Los Angeles Rams

Coach John Robinson said of Eric Dickerson: 'He's on his way to becoming the greatest running back of all time.' Why? The fans could tell you: he's electrified them with his size, speed and sheer strength — a truly winning combination which makes him one of the major offensive forces in the NFL. During 1983 and '84 he averaged an incredible 122 yards per game and better than five yards (5.08) per carry. In both years he was a consensus All-Pro — his 3,913 yards gained during those first two seasons is the most ever in NFL history. 1984 was, for Dickerson, a great year; he had 12 100-yard games — an NFL record. He also set the league record for most total yards from scrimmage with an astounding 2,244 (2,105 rushing, 139 receiving). And of course he hasn't been short of recognition. As a rookie in 1981 he won virtually all rookie of the year honours and a host of national awards; he's also been named NFC player of the year by UPI, *Football News*, *USA Today*, Washington DC Touchdown Club, Columbus Ohio Touchdown Club, Atlanta Touchdown Club and Kansas City Committee of 101; and was NFL most valuable player runner up to Dan Marino.

1986 saw Eric Dickerson crash through the 1,000-yard barrier before anyone else in the NFL. He finished as the league's leading rusher with 1,821 yards and also gained the most yards from scrimmage, 2,026.

Dickerson wears just about every bit of protection he can, from special plastic glasses to a made-to-measure mouth guard. He is an explosive player with the speed of a gazelle and an almost superhuman ability to dodge tackles.

THE BACKROOM BOYS & GIRLS

The stars of each team are obviously the players, the superstars who are seen on network tv, who can earn fortunes from advertising, endorsements, public speaking and so on. But behind each team of players there is a formidable organisation to make sure that the team is run as an efficient, well-oiled, disciplined and happy unit. As an example let's look at the Dallas Cowboys' staff — the non-players — the people who apart from the coaches are never seen but whose job is just as important as any of the players'.

At the very top of the pile there is the Chief Cowboy, HR 'Bum' Bright, general partner, a president and general manager, and three vice-presidents.

Coaching

Tom Landry has been head coach for 27 years — his favourite joke is that in all that time he's never had a promotion! But this former Second World War pilot is quite happy with the situation as one of the most successful coaches in pro football history with teams coached by him among the most often victorious of any coach's teams. Under Landry there are 10 specialist coaches and two secretaries. The specialist coaches concentrate on specific areas of the team — it is Landry who puts it all together.

There is an assistant head coach with responsibility for the offensive line, one for running backs, one for special teams, another for receivers, one for quarterbacks, one for defensive backs, another for the defensive line, one for linebackers, one for 'conditioning' and one more for 'research and development'. All these people are specialists in the particular position. Imagine if in English soccer there was a coach just for centre-forwards!

Scouting

Every professional team is on the lookout for new talent and the Cowboys scouting staff travel the country looking at college players to see if they could ever become future Cowboys. Dallas has no fewer than eight scouts and two secretaries. They spend an enormous amount of time on the road, writing reports on all the young players — all the information is filed on computer for easy reference. They will measure a player's speed, strength and assess his personality — the player's attitude plays a very important part. He may be the fastest thing on two legs with super-glue fingers — but if his attitude is wrong he won't make the team.

A sample questionnaire is set out below.
RUNNING BACK
NAME .... HEIGHT ....
SCHOOL............................. WEIGHT ....
AGE .... DISTANCE.......... TIME ....
MARKS OUT OF 10

HE IS STRONG   _____

HE WANTS TO WIN   _____

HE IS UNSELFISH   _____

HE LISTENS TO ADVICE   _____

HE CAN OVERPOWER A
MAN OF EQUAL STRENGTH   _____

HE RETAINS WHAT
HE HAS LEARNED   _____

HE DOESN'T FUMBLE   _____

HE CAN WORK IN A TEAM   _____

PROSPECTS OF PLAYING PRO
EXCELLENT
V. GOOD
GOOD
SLIM
NONE

Medical

In their medical division the Cowboys employ five different people: a trainer, an assistant trainer and three doctors. Normally at each game two of the doctors are present in case of injury and each doctor is a specialist in his field. They all work full time for the club.

Counselling services

The Cowboys have a full-time counsellor whose job is to look after the players' well-being. If a man has emotional, financial, family or drug problems the counsellor is on call to help.

Photography

Each game is filmed, so are practice sessions, so the players can assess their own performance and the performance of their team mates. The Cowboys employ a director and assistant director for this very important job.

Equipment

Each club has an equipment manager to make sure all equipment is in good order. The Cowboys have a manager and two assistants. Plus on game days 'locker room boys' are brought in to tidy up, put the soiled uniforms in big bins for washing. It's not the most glamorous of jobs, but the kids that do it are at least part of the club, next to their heroes — there is no shortage of 'locker room boys'.

Public relations

All NFL clubs employ public relations staff to cope with the thousands of press, tv and radio interview requests that come in every season. The Cowboys have four people exclusively for this most demanding of jobs.

Cowboys Weekly

The Cowboys have a weekly paper distributed to fans, and to produce this they have an editor, assistant editor, advertising director, production manager, contribution manager, and an advertising assistant and a secretary, plus of course freelance contributors.

Administration

Of course each club is in business to maximise profits and the Cowboys' administration staff see to that. There are 11 of them all told — business manager, controller, building engineer, accounting, secretary, business receptionist, two other secretaries, another accountant and an office aide.

Ticket office

Here the Cowboys have three people, a ticket manager, assistant manager and an assistant to the assistant manager!

Entertainment

Half-time entertainment is a very important part of the game and the Cowboys employ a half-time director and a band director to organise the spectacular half-time shows.

Cheerleaders

The Dallas Cowboys Cheerleaders are known worldwide — not only do they entertain home and away, they have travelled to remote outposts of the world — to American servicemen, to ex-servicemen in hospital and to make regular appearances at state fairs and colleges. For the 1985–6 season there were 36 girls whose vocations ranged from secretaries to students, to a systems analyst to a property manager.

The girls are chaperoned at all professional engagements and there is a very strict rule that they must not fraternise with the players. If they are caught with a player they are immediately fired. There are four people who organise them — a director, an assistant director, and two choreographers.

The Cowboys also have a 28-member band of brass musicians who play at Texas Stadium and who appear at community concerts and conventions.

The Houston Oilers' mascot, a fun extra

Tie all these people together along with the extra security personnel, merchandisers, hot-dog vendors, bar staff, turnstile people, and general 'go-fors' and you can see a typical American football team is a vast and formidable business machine as well.

Fans destroyed so many goalposts in after-match celebrations that now posts are sunk into cement.

It's said that in a nightclub in Ottawa the winner of a $1 lottery gets the chance to throw a brick at a tv screen showing football commentator Howard Cosell's image — business is brisk!

A cheerleader for the Los Angeles Raiders, all part of the razzmatazz of football

COLLEGE FOOTBALL

For anyone with a dream of playing professional football the road starts seriously at college. Scouting organisations and scouts from individual teams systematically and constantly assess college players and the annual draft of college players into professional teams is the road that all professional players follow.

If you are good at a particular sport in the United States it is possible to get a degree without any brains. All you have to do is to play, run, swim, or jump well and a scholarship can be found to get you through college. This is not always the case, however: some of America's top statesmen, generals, doctors, lawyers and businessmen have played college football. The game has also been a breeding ground for US Presidents, of whom Ronald Reagan is the latest in a long line.

College football is big business: in 1985 over 25 million people attended top campus football games, and another 11 million watched the grass roots group of college teams, the same number as attended NFL professional games.

Although it is against the rules for college players to receive money for playing, life is made very comfortable for the top players. In the 1985 Rose Bowl, the college game's most prestigious match, University College Los Angeles and Iowa divided a pot worth $5.6 million.

If the players don't make money while at college, the coaches most certainly do. Paul Bryant, coach of the Alabama Crimson Tide team, is reported to have earned $450,000 in 1981. Back in 1937 when Dana Xenophon Bible became head coach of the Texas Longhorns, he demanded and got a salary of $15,000. The Texas legislature had to vote on it, as it was more than the university president's income.

They paid up but not before they also voted that the president's pay should be increased to match Bible's.

Coaches can be more important than the head of the college. Gil Dobie, who was head coach of the University of Washington in Seattle from 1907 to 1916 had a row with the president after his 1916 team had won the Rose Bowl and quit. The school newspaper reported this dreadful news with the following editorial, 'The disagreement between Dobie and President Suzzalo is caused by a misapprehension on the part of the president. In some manner Suzzalo has gotten the idea that educational functions of the university are of more importance than the football team'.

College football today is made up of regional conferences plus a number of independent teams. This has happened because of the great distances that would have to be travelled if the game was played on a national scale. Teams played their local rivals and this is still the case today.

Conferences

Atlantic Coast
Clemson
Duke
Georgia Tech
Maryland
North Carolina
North Carolina State
Virginia
Wake Forest

Southeastern
Florida
Louisiana
Alabama
Auburn
Georgia

Kentucky
Mississippi
Mississippi State
Tennessee
Vanderbilt
Southwest
Arkansas
Baylor
Houston
Rice
SMU
Texas A&M
Texas Christian
Texas Tech

Big Eight
Colorado
Iowa State
Kansas
Kansas State
Missouri
Nebraska
Oklahoma
Oklahoma State
Big Ten
Illinois
Indiana
Iowa
Michigan
Michigan State
Minnesota
Northwestern
Ohio State
Purdue
Wiscosin
Pac-10
Arizona
Arizona State
California
Oregon
Oregon State
Stanford
UCLA
USC
Washington
Washington State

Bernie Kosar playing for the University of Miami before being recruited into pro football

The Los Angeles Rams once accused the Chicago Bears of tapping their telephone lines — it seems every device is used to win the game!

47

Three other conferences make up the list of the National Collegiate Athletic Association Division 1A: the Mid-American Conference, Western Athletic Conference and the Pacific Coast Athletic Association. In 1985 the Missouri Valley Conference withdrew from Division 1A and will compete in 1-AA competition.

Although the Ivy League contains some of the oldest teams in the game it actually plays in Division 1-AA. This is because of the amount of time that students have to give if their team plays in the premier league.

Ivy League
Brown
Columbia
Cornell
Dartmouth
Harvard
Pennsylvania
Princeton
Yale

Some of the great college teams have never been members of a conference, instead playing all comers. Notre Dame, for example, has not missed conference football, having been voted national champions more times than any other college. And only eight colleges have won the title in consecutive years and this group include two independents, Notre Dame and Army.

The Independents
Army Boston College
Bucknell
Cincinnati
Colgate
Delaware

East Carolina
Florida State
Holy Cross
Lafayette

LeHigh
Louisville

Memphis State
Miami (Florida)
Navy
Northeastern

Notre Dame
Penn State
Pittsburgh
Rutgers

South Carolina
Southern Mississippi
Southwestern Louisiana
Syracuse
Temple
Tennessee State

Tulane
Virginia Tech
West Virginia
William & Mary

Football's Loss . . .

The thirty-fourth President of the USA, Dwight Eisenhower, was once, way back in 1912, a starting halfback for Arms in the Cadets. However, his football career came to an abrupt end that same year when he suffered a major knee injury.

Conrad Dobler (St. Louis Cardinals) once punched the opposition in the head — during a pre-game coin toss! He was voted the NFL's most unpopular player by a large margin.

An on-field celebration by the University College of Los Angeles during a match against Oregon State University

The sacred turf of Wembley Stadium invaded in August 1986 by the Dallas Cowboys and Chicago Bears to play in the American Bowl '86.

AMERICAN FOOTBALL IN BRITAIN

The first reported game of American football in Britain took place in 1910 when teams from two American warships, the USS *Rhode Island* and the USS *Georgia*, played an exhibition game at the Stonebridge ground in Northfleet, Kent. A crowd of over 4,000 turned out on a bitterly cold day to witness the *Georgia's* team win 11–0. The date for the history books was 21 December 1910.

After the Second World War there was an abundance of American serviceman stationed in Britain and service teams played inter-divisional games all over the country. But as a participation sport among the British, the real beginning wasn't until 1982 when Channel 4 television came on the air. The new tv channel's weekly show of American football games effectively lit the fuse. Public reaction exceeded all expectations and these programmes quickly established themselves as a staple part of the armchair sportsfans' diet. Super Bowl XVII, beamed live from the Pasadena Rose Bowl in California in January 1983, was watched by over three million British fans who staved off sleep and sat up until 3 am to watch the Washington Redskins defeat the Miami Dolphins.

It was almost inevitable that a small band of dedicated enthusiasts would want to take the game out of the television and into the park. Such a small band of gridiron followers were soon making a name for themselves on a makeshift pitch in London's Hyde Park. They

AMERICAN Football at Northfleet

COUNCILLOR CHURCH ENTERTAINS THE SAILORS.

Teams from the U.S.S. "Georgia" and "Rhode Island" gave an exhibition game on the Sports Ground on Wednesday before a good attendance. The game is interesting to watch, but "football" seems a misnomer, the feet being very seldom used, while the match seems to be won more by sheer physical strength than by science.

It appears that the "downs" count; the side in possession must get three downs in 10 yards or the ball goes to the opponents. The man with the ball does not receive the sole attention of the players, but every one of his comrades who essays to help him is collared and unceremoniously pushed or knocked out of the way. Should a man get hurt or tired others are ready to take his place. Each man is well padded, even the nose and teeth having guards, and present a peculiar appearance. The period of play is divided into quarters, with an interval between each. In some respects it is not unlike Rugby.

Both teams had a plethora of supporters, each doing their best to urge on their favourites. Rhode Island had the better of the first quarter, and were in a favourable position early in the second, but Georgia then got the grip of their signs and forced them back. Levy, in a smart run, touching down (five points) and being successful in the place kick, increased their score to six points. The Georgia team maintained their superiority in the third quarter, but were unable to increase their lead. The fourth quarter was the hardest contested, Georgia by sheer force pushing their opponents over the line, enabling Levy again to touch down, and eventually securing the maximum points. Thus Georgia were victors by 12 points to nil, Levy, their hero, being carried shoulder high.

At the conclusion of the match, the sailors, to the number of 220, were entertained ...

From the *Gravesend and Dartford Reporter*, 24 December 1910, courtesy of Recorder Newspapers

called themselves the London Ravens. Little did any of them realise that within three years they would become the first British champions. By the summer of 1983 they had acquired some kit from the USA and the first game between British and American sides took place at Stamford Bridge in July when the Ravens went down 8–0 to a team from the USAF base at Chicksands in Bedfordshire. The news of this event travelled fast and soon other teams began to spring up all over the country — in Birmingham a team was forming called the Bulls, in Manchester the Spartans, originally called the Northwich Spartans, were getting equipment and preparing to face the Ravens and teams were forming in all parts of the country from Glasgow in the north to Taunton and Cardiff in the west.

October 1983 marked the first game between two all-British sides. The London Ravens travelled north to play the Northwich Spartans and swamped them 48–0. A return game in the capital resulted in a similar score, and British American football was well and truly under way.

Throughout the winter months attempts were made to form a national league but most foundered. In February 1984 at a meeting in Bedford, 35 teams met to discuss the formation of an association. It was decided to re-convene in two weeks' time to formalise the proposals. At this meeting on 3 March at the headquarters of the Boy Scouts, Baden Powell House in London, not one league but two were formed. Twenty-six clubs were represented and a stormy debate ensued, with two options being offered. The end result was that seven clubs broke away to form the British American Football Federation (BAFF) and the remaining 19 formed the American Football League (UK) (AFLUK).

Headed by a 42-year-old Birmingham-based American, Gerry Hartman, the AFL quickly started to get its act together, but time was short if a season was to happen that summer and the project needed financing. A further meeting of the 19 clubs at USAF Chicksands later in the month got the show on the road and the first AFL game was organised to take place on the Dorset coast on 8 April.

The hometown Poole Sharks faced the Northampton Stormbringers and emerged from a baptism of fire with a stunning 48–0 loss in front of over 3,000 enthusiastic spectators, although the Stormbringers had several experienced Americans in their squad. The game caught the imagination of the whole country. National television news coverage of the event spread the word and teams began springing up at the rate of four or five per week. Within a month the AFL had increased to 28 clubs.

Meanwhile BAFF, the other smaller league, began to organise schedules. Under the leadership of Mike Lytton BAFF kicked off their season on 21 July when the Ealing Eagles beat the Crawley Raiders 20–0.

At varying dates clubs opened what would be for them a season of exhibition games designed to launch this new and exciting sport on an unsuspecting British public.

One bit of unfair play

Each home team has to provide its visiting opponent with essentials like locker rooms, medical equipment, and protein drinks plus, of course, the bench. The home side gets to choose which side of the field they sit on, so in a hot climate the home side will opt for the bench in the shade and make their opponents sit in the blazing sun, and in cold weather the home team will make their opponents sit on the least protected side of the field where the wind can cut like a knife.

The Fylde Falcons and the Tyneside Trojans battle it out within sight of that great English institution, the Blackpool Tower

American football being played against an unmistakably English background

The Milton Keynes Bucks began their history with a classical local derby game with the Northampton Stormbringers' team in June. Over 7,000 paying fans watched in glorious sunshine as the Bucks came from behind to defeat the Stormbringers 20–18. A missed field goal with only two seconds left on the clock cost the Northampton team their unbeaten record.

But with any new sport there were the inevitable teething problems. Teams couldn't find enough officials, the national press were not that interested. Newspapers and tv stations were treating the new sport as a 'news' item, something different. Many likened it to the short-lived skateboarding craze that had gone before.

In April 1984 there were just four teams who had spent over £7,000 to buy equipment to play the game. Within a month that number had risen to ten and by the time NFL football came back to the television screens in the September there were at least 40.

American football was beginning to be appreciated. Nearly 4,000 fans attended the Birmingham Bulls' first game with the Bucks at the Alexander Stadium in July 1984; a crowd estimated at 3,000 watched the Heathrow Jets go down to the Poole Sharks, and some 2,500 witnessed the Glasgow Lions host the Manchester Spartans in the nation's first venture on to AstroTurf.

The London Ravens, victors of the first Summer Bowl, the British game's 'Super Bowl', played in August 1985

That first season had no official end. Most of the clubs wanted to keep on playing throughout the winter, trying to gain as much playing expertise as possible before the first championship schedule for both AFL and BAFF leagues in 1985. During those winter months teams all over the UK played games and 'controlled scrimmage' practices; a series of meetings was held with the aim of bringing the two leagues together, and a referees' association set up. The British American Football Referees' Association (BAFRA) was the brainchild of former soccer official Dave Norton and by the end of 1984 the association had well over 100 members. Aided by officials from the USAF training seminars were held and BAFRA was up and running.

The winter meetings between the two leagues, however, did not prove fruitful. A conference in Birmingham organised by Mike Sheppard, a local council official, gained much publicity, with all the senior league members attending but, as had happened at the previous meeting, it didn't bring about the required unity. What happened in fact was the birth of another, third league. The United Kingdom American Football Association was headed by Sheppard and ran for only one year. Probably the most closely guarded meeting between the two main leagues — AFL and BAFF — took place in a run-down cafe on the edge of the city's famous Bullring shopping centre after one of the Birmingham conferences. Drinking mugs of tea and munching bacon sandwiches, officials of

William 'The Refrigerator' Perry
Chicago Bears

Only in pop music and American football can people become superstars overnight. One day he was William Perry . . . 'The Fridge', the next he was '*The* Refrigerator' appearing on tv talk shows, making tv commercials, drawing the crowds in their droves, and had his *own* set of cheerleaders. He was signed up by one of the biggest and most powerful management companies to administer the fortune he was making . . . The Fridge had arrived.

He got his nickname while he was playing college football at Clemson University in South Carolina not just because of his size, but because as legend has it he could eat the entire contents of a fridge in one go. He came to the notice of the Chicago Bears in the spring of 1985 when their head coach Mike Ditka saw him at a testing ground in Arizona. He weighed over 25 stone but despite this enormous weight, Ditka was impressed. After all, in his first two games at Clemson in his senior year he was the best player on the field. Ditka wanted him but the Bears' defensive coach Buddy Ryan was very much against drafting Perry.

'He's nothing but a fat kid, a wasted draft choice, a waste of money.' But Ditka knew that if Perry could control his weight he would be a tremendous asset to the team.

Ditka was right and on 21 October 1985 against the Green Bay Packers Perry proved that 'fat is beautiful.' First he led Walter Payton in for a touchdown — then he scored himself, then with an awesome block he led Payton through for another touchdown.

Perry has worked hard to control his weight and despite his enormous success he still has his large feet very firmly on the ground. He realises that the tv commercials won't go on for ever and that he has to be a footballer first and a star second.

When the Chicago Bears played the Dallas Cowboys at Wembley in August 1986 'The Fridge' caught the imagination of the British public too — he became an overnight celebrity, appearing on talk shows and featuring in numerous newspaper articles.

In Mike Ditka's autobiography he says of Perry: 'If he diets, controls himself and gets into the weight room, like he has to, it will be interesting. His wife is a help too. You are what you eat. If you eat everything in sight, you'll be everything in sight!'

I think Perry has a great future ahead of him and I'll leave the last word to coach Ditka who says,

'People who don't think Perry is a good football player should have their heads examined.'

both leagues tried to come to a compromise solution. It didn't work and 1985 saw three leagues in operation.

At the beginning of the 1985 season the AFL had 40 members, all fully equipped to play tackle football and ready to start a gruelling 16-week programme of games. BAFF had picked up nicely since the previous autumn and its membership stood at some 20 clubs, although only half of them had kit. The star team of that season was undoubtedly the London Ravens. They waltzed through the regular season unbeaten and then proceeded to see off Oxford and Leicester in the play-offs before meeting the Streatham Olympians in the first official final — the Summer Bowl.

Officials of the league had wanted to call it the 'UK Super Bowl', but the NFL in New York would not agree, so the name Summer Bowl was dreamed up by the League's media director Peter Rowe. A venue for such a prestigious final had also to be found. Twickenham's hallowed rugby field seemed interested but later backed out. Eventually with the aid of a sponsor an agreement was signed with Aston Villa soccer club and the first Summer Bowl took place at Villa Park on 26 August 1985.

The Birmingham Bulls were another fancied contender for a final berth. They had also gone through the regular season unbeaten and ended up as Central division winners. In the play-offs they beat Greenwich and then faced the Glasgow Lions, late replacements for the Tyneside Trojans who were unable to field a team because of a crippling injury list.

The semi-final tie at Oxford proved to be one of the hardest games of the year. Birmingham were the clear pre-game favourites, but Streatham, a fit and strong team, upset the odds and emerged as 13–12 winners. A last-minute drive from the Bulls to save the game resulted in wide receiver Maverick Logan being called for out of bounds when it looked as if he had caught the all-important game-winning touchdown.

The Summer Bowl final never really lived up to its pre-game predictions. Many had hoped for a head-to-head clash between these two London teams, the Ravens and Olympians, but in the end the Ravens confirmed their superiority with a superb 45–7 victory. In front of an estimated 10,000 crowd the Ravens opened up a big lead with scoring runs from Ebubedike and Cruz before most valuable player Joe St. Louis waltzed some 70 yards to crown the day for the big black shadow. The Summer Bowl had turned out to be a good day for football, but before the kick-off it was fraught with problems. A task force of six league officials had worked day and night for six weeks. They had tried to overcome every possible obstacle. The fact that they got the event off the ground at all is a credit to their efforts.

But even before the game the dark rumour clouds that had threatened American football before it had even had a chance to get itself properly organised began to loom overhead. Talk of a new league, the fourth, was uppermost in everybody's minds. Some clubs had already openly stated what their intentions were. Others were not so sure. The rumours of a new league — the Budweiser League — were stronger when BAFF staged their championship final in London in October. The Rockingham Rebels came to town and did a demolition job on the Croydon Coyotes, 13–0.

 *Football's Loss . . .*

Remember the character Joe Coffey in tv's *Hill Street Blues*? Once recognisable in the purple, gold and white colours of the Minnesota Vikings, Ed Marinaro became better known for the blue uniform of Police Officer Coffey. He last wore football colours in 1977 as a short-term member of the Seattle Seahawks.

American footballers and a Union Jack? An unheard of combination a few years ago, it's becoming a more common sight as the game catches on in Britain.

Two weeks earlier the first international game took place at Walton-on-Thames where a strong British squad overcame the more experienced French by a 7–0 scoreline. The season for all intents and purposes was now at an end. Football was over for another year, and the politics were about to begin.

American Brewers Anheuser Busch had decided that they wanted to sponsor a league, but after failing to agree terms with either AFL or BAFF, they went their own way. Their European Sales Director Harry Drnec declared defiantly, 'We are going to play football next year.' They did.

Because of the threat from Budweiser, the AFL and BAFF decided to bury the hatchet and merge. The new league, to be called BAFL, was officially announced at the BAFF final in October. AFL Chairman Terry Clark, recently elected to replace the outgoing Gerry Hartman, met with BAFF's Mike Lytton in a series of meetings and the full plan was put to the membership in Leicester later in the month.

Budweiser held their first meeting a week later, an open meeting for all interested clubs. From that first presentation it was obvious that they meant business and within a month they were claiming over 50 teams. BAFL were doing likewise. A war of words then erupted between the two leagues as the propaganda was sent out in reams. One side claiming this, the other claiming something else. Football was in total disarray.

The London Ravens and the Streatham Olympians announced that they were switching from the old AFL to join Budweiser, and by Christmas it was obvious that Budweiser had the bigger of the two rival factions. The war of words erupted into verbal abuse in March when the Streatham Olympians were told that their attractive pre-season match with the Dusseldorf Panthers would not go ahead.

BAFL was the only league that the EFL, the sports governing body in Europe, would recognise. None of the Budweiser teams was to be allowed to play in Europe. Telexes and letters of protest from both sides did not lead to a peaceful solution.

The Manchester Allstars took the Olympians' place in a game in Boulogne before Christmas after the Olympians had been told that they would not be welcome because they did not play in the right league. The Allstars took their place and won the game.

Right leagues or wrong leagues, the new season was approaching fast and much had to be done. Thankfully the war quietened down as 27 April, the start of the new season, approached.

A month before, at Leicester in freezing conditions, the Birmingham Bulls and the Leicester Panthers met for the right to take the Ravens' place in the first European championships. The Bulls emerged victors and represented BAFL in Amsterdam in August with seven teams from the other EFL member countries.

The new season, with more teams playing than ever before, opened to much ballyhoo. But as far as results were concerned it was the same as the previous year. The Ravens continued to dominate their league, conceding only one touchdown in their first six games. The Bulls and the Panthers were taking their opposition to the cleaners as they romped away in a two horse race for the BAFL title, although hot on their heels were the Milton Keynes Bucks and the Nottingham Hoods.

The Hoods had acquired an American running back from the University of Illinois — Clifton Stroughter. Stroughter was a room mate of New England Patriots quarterback Tony Eason at school, but now he was tearing up the records in British football. In his opening game he was ejected for arguing with officials, but soon made up for that disappointment with touchdown runs that set the whole football community talking. Six against Portsmouth, then eight against another team. The introduction of several classy American players into both leagues improved the standard of play for many teams.

In June the London Ravens, previously a solely British team, changed their attitude and signed up quarterback Ron Riberts, who had recently had a try-out with the Pittsburgh Steelers. The Ravens were still unbeaten as they marched onward to another perfect season.

Phil Ambrose, a 24-year-old running back from South Stat Scorpions, became the first player to reach the magical 1,000 yards mark and Thames Valley Chargers' American quarterback Ron Dubie reached it for passing on 22 June in a win over the Heathrow Jets.

1986 saw new standards and new records, as the game continued to grow in this country. During the close season, amid much speculation of a merger, the BAFL collapsed.

When the 1987 season kicked off, there was a single league under the Budweiser banner comprising teams from both the old Budweiser league and the BAFL. There were some 150 applications for membership, with 105 clubs eventually included in the new structure.

A new governing body was also set up, called the British American Football Association (BAFA). The new Budweiser League comprised three divisions, with a system of promotion and relegation eventually to be introduced. Four conferences of five teams formed the National Division and with the best teams in the country divided on a broadly geographical basis, this was designed to be the league's flagship. National Division teams contested the new showpiece of the British game, the Bud Bowl.

Six conferences made up the Premier Division, whose 10-game season culminated in the Premier Bowl. The remaining 49 clubs made up Division One and were divided among eight conferences.

In a system designed to raise standards and public awareness, it was hoped that the promise of regular football of the highest quality, particularly in the National Division, would attract large numbers of spectators through the gate.

THE TEAMS

Seattle Seahawks

Minnesota Vikings

Gree

San Francisco 49ers

Denver Broncos

Los Angeles Raiders

Kansas City Chiefs

Los Angeles Rams

St Louis Cardin

San Diego Chargers

Dallas Cowboys

New Orleans S

Houston Oilers

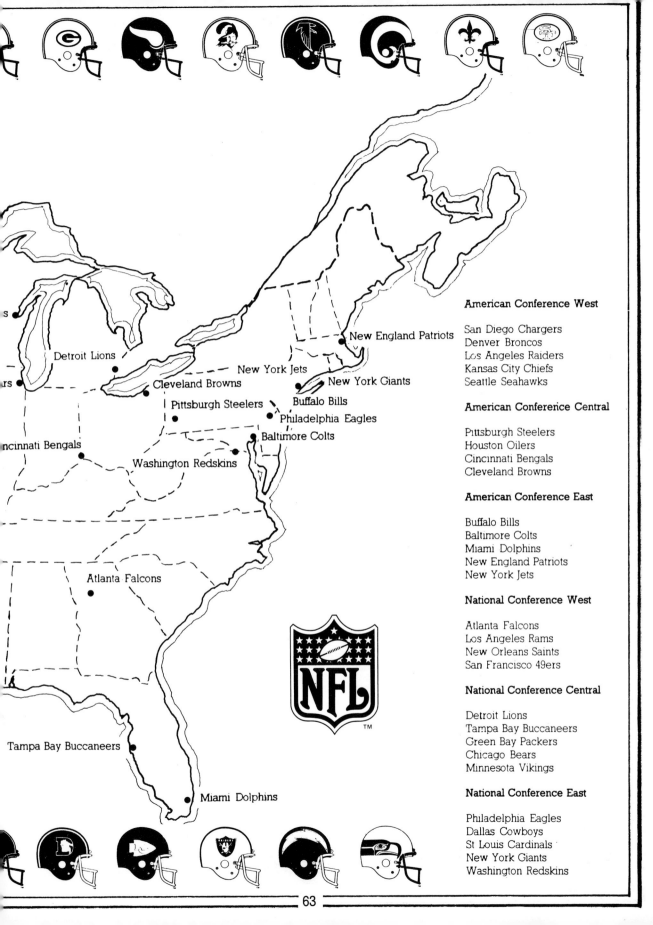

American Conference West

San Diego Chargers
Denver Broncos
Los Angeles Raiders
Kansas City Chiefs
Seattle Seahawks

American Conference Central

Pittsburgh Steelers
Houston Oilers
Cincinnati Bengals
Cleveland Browns

American Conference East

Buffalo Bills
Baltimore Colts
Miami Dolphins
New England Patriots
New York Jets

National Conference West

Atlanta Falcons
Los Angeles Rams
New Orleans Saints
San Francisco 49ers

National Conference Central

Detroit Lions
Tampa Bay Buccaneers
Green Bay Packers
Chicago Bears
Minnesota Vikings

National Conference East

Philadelphia Eagles
Dallas Cowboys
St Louis Cardinals
New York Giants
Washington Redskins

New England Patriots
Detroit Lions
New York Jets
Cleveland Browns
New York Giants
Pittsburgh Steelers
Buffalo Bills
Philadelphia Eagles
Baltimore Colts
Cincinnati Bengals
Washington Redskins
Atlanta Falcons
Tampa Bay Buccaneers
Miami Dolphins

Atlanta Falcons

1–85 Suwanee Road, Suwanee, Georgia 30174
(404) 261 5400

Stadium: Atlanta-Fulton County Stadium, 521 Capitol Avenue SW, Atlanta, Georgia 30312. 60,748 capacity; grass.

Conference: NFC (Western Division)

Colours: red, black, silver and white

1965 Rivalry between the NFL and AFL to establish an expansion team in Atlanta results in Atlanta being the first city able to choose which league to join. The citizens opt for the NFL.

The franchise is bought by Rankin M. Smith, the vice-president of an insurance company, for about $8.5 million.

The team's nickname is chosen via a local radio contest; the winner asserts that the falcon is a 'proud bird full of courage and fight'.

1968 The team's uniforms are changed by the elimination of the black falcon emblem from jersey sleeves, to be replaced by stripes.

Head coach Norb Hecker is replaced by Norm Van Brocklin, previously with the Minnesota Vikings. Under the latter's direction, the Falcons break an 11-game losing streak with a win over the New York Giants on 13 October.

1969 With Van Brocklin's new staff, the Falcons have their best-ever season: 6–8–0.

1970 Van Brocklin takes over as general manager in addition to his coaching responsibilities.

1971 The Falcons' uniform is altered again — from black to red jerseys.

1973 In their opening game, the Falcons set 35 team records during their massive defeat — 62–7 — of the New Orleans Saints.

1974 Due to the team's lack of wins, Van Brocklin is fired mid-season and replaced as head coach by Marion Campbell.

The Falcons gain the dubious record of 40,202 'no-shows' (people who do not attend the game, despite having tickets) for their game against the Los Angeles Rams on 1 December — they lost, 30–7. They beat this record two weeks later with 48,830 no-shows in a rain-swept victory over the Green Bay Packers.

1976 Campbell is sacked and general manager Pat Peppler takes over. However, after a humiliating defeat at the hands of the Los Angeles Rams — 59–0 — he, too, is relieved of duty, to be succeeded the following year by Eddie LeBaron as general manager and Leeman Bennett as head coach.

1978 Once again, the uniform is changed, but it has remained the same ever since.

The Falcons have their first winning season since 1973: 9–7–0. This results in a wild card place in the divisional play-offs, where they lose to the Dallas Cowboys.

1980 Western Division champions.

1982 The Falcons participate in the play-offs, but lose their first game to the Minnesota Vikings, 30–24.

1984 Englishman Mick Luckhurst — a kicker — becomes the team's all-time leading scorer on 9 September.

Gerald Riggs

1986 Dan Henning sacked as coach. Star running back Gerald Riggs gains his third consecutive 1,000-yard season and a late place in the Pro Bowl.

★ ★ ★ ★ ★ ★ ★ ★ ★ ★ ★ ★ ★ ★

Buffalo Bills

1 Bills Drive, Orchard Park, New York 14127
(716) 648 1800

Stadium: Rich Stadium (*address as above*). 80,290 capacity; AstroTurf.

Conference: AFC (Eastern Division)

Colours: scarlet, white and royal blue

1959 Ralph C. Wilson, a shareholder in the Detroit Lions, is awarded a franchise to establish an AFL team in Buffalo.

1960 Over 100,000 Buffalo citizens turn out to meet the Bills as they return from training camp before their first pre-season game.

1962 Running back Cookie Gilchrist becomes the AFL's first 1,000-yard runner.

1964 AFL champions, defeating the San Diego Chargers.

1965 After demanding more money following the previous year's championship season, Gilchrist is traded to the Denver Broncos.

Mick Luckhurst, who hails from England, the Falcons' top-class kicker

AFL champions, again defeating the San Diego Chargers.

1966 Eastern Division champions.

1969 After intense negotiations, Heisman Trophy winner O. J. 'The Juice' Simpson is signed to a long-term contract.

1971 After the Bills win only one game that season, Lou Saban (who had previously coached the team, 1962–5) rejoins as head coach and 'vice-president in charge of football'.

1972 Saban proceeds to rebuild the Bills. After two disappointing seasons O. J. Simpson begins to live up to his potential and is named AFC player of the year.

1973 The Bills move into Orchard Park stadium (later renamed Rich Stadium) from their old stamping grounds at the War Memorial Stadium.
The team becomes the first in AFL history to run for more than 3,000 yards.

1976 Simpson insists on being traded to the Los Angeles Rams but later signs a

☆ Football's Loss . . .

Jack Kemp

American football, a game all about strategy and tactics, has certainly nurtured its fair share of politicians. Among them, Jack Kemp, the man who quarterbacked the Los Angeles Rams and San Diego Chargers to AFL divisional titles in 1960 and 1961, and the Buffalo Bills to AFL championships in 1964 and 1965. What's he up to now? Since 1971 he's been a member of the United States House of Representatives and he is now being groomed as a democratic contender for the Presidency. There's been an ex-actor as President — why not an ex-footballer?

The Buffalo Bills playing the New York Jets

three-year contract worth more than $2 million to stay with the Bills.

After three losses in the first five games of the season, Saban resigns 'in the best interests of the team'.

1977 Simpson is benched with a knee injury for half the season.

1978 Simpson is traded to the San Francisco 49ers.

1980 Eastern Division champions.

1983 Coach Chuck Knox replaced by Kay Stephenson.

1985 Kay Stephenson replaced by Hank Bullough.

1986 Former Kansas City coach Marv Levy signs a 'multi-year' contract to replace Hank Bullough, sacked mid-way through another indifferent season. Levy becomes the Bills' third coach in 13 months. Within three weeks the team ends a 22-game losing streak on the road, with a 17–14 victory over Levy's former team, the Chiefs.

Hall of Fame member

O. J. Simpson: running back, 1969–77

The great OJ Simpson, running back with the Buffalo Bills from 1969 to 1977 and a 1985 entrant to the Hall of Fame

What do the Russians think about American football? Sovietskii Sport said:
'It is impossible not to shudder at the players' cruelty . . . any of them can commit an act of cruelty, but only a handful can do it before 60,000 people without being detected.'

Chicago Bears

Halas Hall, 250 North Washington, Lake Forest, Illinois 60045
(312) 295–6600

Stadium: Soldier Field, 425 McFetridge Place, Chicago, Illinois 60605. 65,793 capacity; AstroTurf.

Conference: NFC (Central Division)

Colours: orange, navy blue and white

1920 Team founded in Decatur, Illinois by starch manufacturer A. E. Staley as a company team, and run by employee George Halas on company time. Halas's favourite play is the T-formation.
Co-champions of the then American Professional Football Association

1921 Because of the business recession, Staley withdraws sponsorship and Halas becomes co-owner with former schoolmate Dutch Sternaman. They move the team to Chicago, where they play at Cub Park, the stadium of the city's baseball team, the Chicago Cubs. Team known as the 'Chicago Staleys' for one year, after their former sponsor pays $5,000 for the privilege.
APFA champions.

1922 Team renamed 'Chicago Bears' to show relationship with the baseball team in whose stadium they play.

1925 Halas signs Red Grange on 22 November, the day after the latter left the University of Illinois, to play for the Bears for the rest of the season; in return, Grange receives a large share of the gate. By the end of January 1926 Grange and his agent C. C. Pyle each earn $100,000.

1926 When Halas refuses to pay Grange a five-figure salary and give him one-third ownership of the Bears, Pyle starts the American Football League and Grange leaves to join an AFL team, the New York Yankees. (He returns to the Bears in 1929, retiring as a member of the team in 1934.)

1930 Sternaman and Halas argue, and Halas steps down as coach and retires as a player, while remaining co-owner.

1932 NFL champions, defeating Portsmouth (Ohio) Spartans. The game is played indoors in the 80-yard-long Chicago Stadium because of Chicago's notorious icy winter temperatures.
Because of the team's financial losses, Sternaman sells his share of the team to Halas for $38,000; Halas is now full owner.

1933 NFL champions, defeating the New York Giants.

1934 Beattie Feathers becomes first back to gain 1,000 yards.
Runners-up in the NFL championship.

1937 Western Division champions.

1940 NFL champions, defeating the Washington Redskins with a record score of 73–0.

1941 NFL champions, defeating the New York Giants. The Bears are now known as the 'Monsters of the Midway'.

1942 Western Division champions, despite losing many players to the armed services, including Halas to the US Navy.

1943 NFL champions, defeating the Washington Redskins.

1946 NFL champions, defeating the New York Giants; many pre-world-war stars have returned to the team.

1956 George Halas retires as head coach. Runners-up in the NFL championship.

1958 George Halas returns as head coach.

1963 NFL champions, defeating the New York Giants.

1968 George Halas, aged 73, retires as head coach, after 40 years of coaching and a record of 320 wins, 147 defeats and 30 draws.

1969 Bears finish last in the league, having won only once in 14 games — their poorest record since they were founded almost 50 years before.

1971 The team moves to Soldier Field.

1982 Mike Ditka becomes head coach.

1983 George 'Papa Bear' Halas dies, aged 88.

1984 Central Division champions.

1986 Central Division champions for the third consecutive season. William 'The Refrigerator' Perry is fined $38,000 in contract bonuses for being overweight. Walter Payton has a record tenth 1,000-yard season and also becomes the first player to gain 20,000 yards in combined rushing and catching.

Hall of Fame members

Doug Atkins: end, 1955–66
George Blanda: quarterback, 1949–58
Dick Butkus: linebacker, 1965–73
Guy Chamberlin: end, 1920–1
George Connor: tackle, 1948–55
John 'Paddy' Driscoll: halfback, 1920, 1926–9

Soldier Field, the Bears' ground and the oldest pro football stadium, opened in 1926

Danny Fortmann: guard, 1936–43
Bill George: linebacker, 1952–65
Red Grange: back, 1925, 1929–34
George Halas: end, 1920–9, coach, 1920–42, 1946–55, 1956–67
Ed Healey: tackle, 1922–7
Bill Hewitt: end, 1932–6
Walt Kiesling: guard, 1934
Bobby Layne: quarterback, 1948
Sid Luckman: quarterback, 1939–50
Roy 'Link' Lyman: tackle, 1926–8, 1930–1, 1933–4
George McAfee: halfback, 1940–1, 1945–50
George Musso: guard, 1933–44
Bronko Nagurski: back, 1930–7, 1943
Gale Sayers: running back, 1965–71
Joe Stydahar: tackle, 1936–42, 1945–6
George Trafton: centre, 1920–32
Clyde 'Bulldog' Turner: centre, 1940–52

Cincinnati Bengals

200 Riverfront Stadium, Cincinnati, Ohio 45202
(513) 621 3550

Stadium: Riverfront Stadium. 59,794 capacity; AstroTurf.

Conference: AFC (Central Division)

Colours: black, orange and white

1967 The AFL franchise for Cincinnati is awarded to a group headed by Paul Brown, former head coach of the Cleveland Browns. As previous Cincinnati

Tight end Rodney Holman

Quarterback Boomer Esiason

Running back Larry Kinnebrew

AFL teams had taken the name of 'Bengals' in 1927, 1930 and 1931, Brown chooses it for his team too.

1969 At the end of the Bengals' second season, with a 4–9–1 record, Brown is named AFL coach of the year.

1970 Central Division champions — a remarkable recovery from being in last place after the first seven games.

1973 Central Division champions.

1976 Paul Brown retires after 41 years as coach; Bill Johnson succeeds him. Brown remains owner, vice-president and general manager.

1978 Johnson resigns after five consecutive losses (but two previous seasons close to the top of the division); he is followed by Homer Rice.

1979 By repeating the 1978 season record of 4–12, Rice is fired and eventually replaced by Forrest Gregg — like Paul Brown, a former Cleveland Browns coach.

1981 The team adopts new uniform with tiger stripes on helmets, jerseys and trousers. Central Division champions.

1982 AFC champions, defeating the San Diego Chargers in appalling weather —

a wind chill factor of minus 59°F.
Defeated in Super Bowl XVI by the San Francisco 49ers.

1985 Finished second in AFC Central Division.

Hall of Fame member

Paul Brown: coach, 1968–75

★ ★ ★ ★ ★ ★ ★ ★ ★ ★ ★ ★ ★ ★ ★

Cleveland Browns

Tower B, Cleveland Stadium, Cleveland, Ohio 44114
(216) 696 5555

Stadium: Cleveland Stadium, West 3rd Street, Cleveland, Ohio 44114. 80,098 capacity; grass.

Conference: AFC (Central Division)

Colours: seal brown, orange and white

1946 Entrepreneur Arthur 'Mickey' McBride wins a franchise for a Cleveland team from the newly formed All-America Football Conference.
Paul Brown is appointed head coach and general manager. In a contest to choose the team's name 36 entrants plump for 'Panthers'. However, coach Brown rejects the name as it was used by a signally unsuccessful NFL Cleveland team in the 1920s. The majority of the other entrants had chosen 'the Browns' — after the new team's just-appointed coach — and after initially refusing to accept this honour, Brown relents and the Browns become the only team ever to be named after its coach. The first player Brown signs is Otto Graham, who will become one of the greatest T-formation quarterbacks in football history.
AAFC champions, defeating the New York Yankees.

1947 AAFC champions, again defeating the New York Yankees.

1948 AAFC champions, defeating the Buffalo Bills after an unbeaten season.

1949 AAFC champions, defeating the San Francisco 49ers.
The AAFC folds, helped to its death by the Browns who, being such dominant champions, caused fans to avoid games which they assumed had foregone conclusions.

1950 The Cleveland Browns are transferred into the NFL.
NFL champions, defeating the Los Angeles Rams.

1951 Eastern Conference champions.

1952 Eastern Conference champions.

1953 McBride sells the team for $600,000 to a syndicate headed by Cleveland industrialist David Jones. They take out a large life assurance policy on coach Paul Brown, regarding him as their most important asset.
Eastern Conference champions.

1954 NFL champions, defeating the Detroit Lions, 56–10. In the game, after which he plans to retire, Otto Graham scores three times, as well as throwing three touchdown passes.

1955 After four games, Brown is aware of a yawning gap without Graham, and he persuades him to return.
Eastern Conference champions.
NFL champions, defeating the Los Angeles Rams. Graham scores twice and makes two touchdown passes, before finally retiring at the end of the game, following a standing ovation by

Bernie Kosar, a great quarterback in the making

all 85,000 fans at the Los Angeles Memorial Coliseum.

1956 The Browns have their first losing season: 5–7–0.

1957 Even though the Browns are only sixth in the queue for the collegiate draft, Paul Brown is fortunate enough to choose Jim Brown, who will prove to be one of the most valuable running backs in NFL history.
Eastern Division champions.

1958 Paul Brown's relationship with his players begins to deteriorate, particularly that with Jim Brown, quarterback Milt Plum and running back Bobby Mitchell.

1961 Former New York advertising executive Arthur Modell buys the Browns for $3,925,000. With his experience in television, he aims to make the team tops in entertainment value — an innovative attitude at the time.

1962 Quarterback Plum is traded, as is Bobby Mitchell, the latter for Syracuse University back Ernie Davis; however, tragically, Davis discovers he is dying of leukaemia.
Jim Brown threatens to retire unless Paul Brown is replaced as coach.

1963 Modell fires Paul Brown, who has been coach and general manager of the Browns for 17 years with a record of 158 victories, 48 defeats and 8 ties. However, his abrasive manner and habit of calling plays from the sidelines via messenger guards has finally beaten him, and he is replaced by his trusted assistant Blanton Collier, whose manner is the exact opposite of Brown's.

1964 NFL champions, defeating the Baltimore Colts.

1965 Eastern Conference champions.
Jim Brown retires.

1967 Century Division champions.

1968 Eastern Conference champions.

1970 The team is transferred to the AFC Central Division.

1971 Central Division champions.

1974 For the first time since 1956, the Browns have a losing season (4–10–0).

1975 Forrest Gregg is named head coach.

1977 Despite an improvement in the team's fortunes the previous year, a losing season (6–8–0) — partially due to injuries — results in Gregg's resignation.

1979 With Sam Rutigliano as head coach, the Browns become known as the 'Kardiac Kids' when 12 out of 16 of their games are cliffhangers as well as victories.

1980 Central Division champions.

1984 Marty Schottenheimer, a former Browns' assistant coach, replaces Sam Rutigliano.

1986 Central Division champions.
Bernie Kosar becomes the first Brown to pass for more than 400 yards twice in his career. He also becomes the first player in NFL history to throw for more than 400 yards without gaining a touchdown.

Hall of Fame members

Doug Atkins: defensive end, 1953–4
Jim Brown: running back, 1957–65
Paul Brown: coach, 1946–63
Willie Davis: defensive end, 1958–9
Len Ford: defensive end, 1950–7
Otto Graham: quarterback, 1946–55
Lou 'The Toe' Groza: tackle/kicker, 1946–59, 1961–7
Marion Motley: back, 1946–53
Dante Lavelli: end, 1946–56
Bill Willis: guard, 1946–53

Left: **running back Kevin Mack**

Above: **running back Earnest Byner**

Dallas Cowboys

1 Cowboy Parkway, Irving, Texas 75063
(214) 556 9900

Stadium: Texas Stadium, Irving, Texas 75062. 65,101 capacity; Texas Turf.

Conference: NFC (Eastern Division)

Colours: royal blue, metallic blue, white

1960 The team is founded with 36 players from other NFL teams and Tom Landry as coach. They play at the Cotton Bowl.

1964 Landry signs a ten-year contract — at that time, the longest contract of any coach in any professional sport.

1967 Runners-up for NFL championship, losing 34–27 to Green Bay Packers on New Year's Day. The game was one of the most exciting in NFL history, with both sides battling it out to the limits of their endurance.

1970 Eastern Division champions.

1971 NFC champions, defeating the San Francisco 49ers.
The team moves to Texas Stadium.

1972 NFC champions, defeating the San Francisco 49ers.
Super Bowl VI champions, defeating the Miami Dolphins.

1973 The Cowboys celebrate their 100th NFL win — over the New Orleans Saints, 40–3.

1976 NFC champions, defeating the Los Angeles Rams. Roger Staubach throws four touchdown passes to clinch the victory.

1978 NFC champions, defeating the Minnesota Vikings.
Super Bowl XII champions, defeating the Denver Broncos.

1979 NFC champions, defeating the Los Angeles Rams.
The team releases a film of the season's highlights entitled *America's Team* — and the nickname has stuck.

1981 NFC East champions.

1984 Missed play-offs for first time for ten years.

1986 Tom Landry receives death threats during the game against the LA Rams. He is escorted from the field by police, but returns to the sidelines in the fourth quarter wearing a bullet-proof vest.
The Cowboys have a losing season for the first time in 20 years.

Hall of Fame members

Herb Adderley: cornerback, 1970–2
Lance Alworth: wide receiver, 1970–1
Forrest Gregg: guard/tackle, 1971
Bob Lilly: defensive end/defensive tackle, 1961–74
Roger Staubach: quarterback, 1969–79

Danny White, Cowboys' quarterback, in action against the Los Angeles Rams

In 1950 the Rams signed an agreement with Admiral TV which stipulated that any loss to the club caused by tv would have to be made up by the sponsoring advertiser — Admiral ended up paying some $300,000!

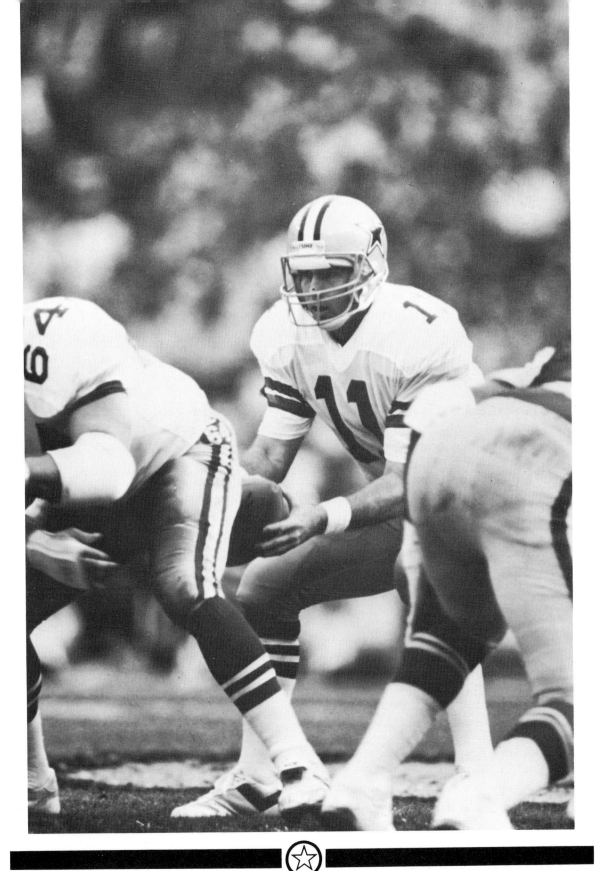

Denver Broncos

5700 Logan Street, Denver, Colorado 80216
(303) 296 1982

Stadium: Mile High Stadium, 1900 West Eliot, Denver, Colorado 80204. 75,100 capacity; grass.

Conference: AFC (Western Division)

Colours: orange, blue and white

1959 The Broncos, with Bob Howsam and his father Lee as majority shareholders, are formed and become charter members of the AFC.

1960 Frank Filchock is appointed as first head coach.
The team has to play in the Bears' baseball stadium, which has limited seating capacity. However, they are watched by 18,372 as they beat the Oakland Raiders in their first home game.
After a losing first season — 4–9–1 — attendances dwindle to 5,861 at the last home game of the year.

1961 The Howsams sell out to a new group headed by Cal Kunz and Gerry Phipps. After an even worse season's record (3–11–0), Filchock is fired.

1962 Jack Faulkner is appointed head coach and general manager.
Faulkner changes the team's uniform from brown and gold to orange, blue and white, and eliminates the vertically striped socks — hated by team and public alike. A pair of the latter are symbolically burned at a public ceremony. With wins over the San Diego Chargers and Houston Oilers and a 7–7–0 record, attendances at home games are more than doubled.

1963 Fielding a team including 14 rookies, the Broncos end the season with a 2–11–1 record.

1964 Winless after four games, when the Broncos lose a fifth to the Boston Patriots, Faulkner is fired and his place is taken by Mac Speedie.

1965 Part-owner Cal Kunz and his supporters sell the team to the Cox Broadcasting Corporation, who plan to transfer it to Atlanta. Gerry and Alan Phipps, who own 42 per cent of the club, decide that it should remain in Denver and buy out the other shareholders for $1.5 million. The threatened removal of the team does wonders for ticket sales as public support for the Broncos snowballs, and before the beginning of the season, season ticket sales reach an all-time high of 22,000.

1966 Relations between coach Speedie and fullback Cookie Gilchrist, who arrived from the Buffalo Bills the previous year, reach rock bottom and Gilchrist is traded, with detrimental effects on the team. One week into the season, Speedie is fired.
Late in the year, Lou Saban is named coach and general manager.

1967 In a pre-season game against the Detroit Lions the Broncos become the first AFL team to defeat an NFL side.

1968 With a new $1.8 million upper level increasing capacity to 50,000, Bears' Stadium is given as a gift to the city of Denver by a non-profit fund-raising group. Its name is officially changed to the 'Denver Mile High Stadium'.

1969 A disappointing 5–8–1 season is highlighted by the Broncos' first-ever shutout of another team — the San Diego Chargers.

Defensive end Rulon Jones

1971 After nine lacklustre games Saban resigns as head coach, following this a month later with his resignation as general manager.

1972 John Ralston of Stanford University is appointed head coach.
Because all season tickets (over 46,500 of them) are already held, there is, for the first time in the Broncos' history, no public sale of season tickets.

1976 With the Mile High Stadium expanded to a 63,500 capacity, season ticket sales are halted at 62,215 — the club's seventh sell-out season.
The team's 9–5–0 record is their best ever.

John Elway
Denver Broncos

Everyone seems to know the story of how a precocious young quarterback called John Elway refused to play for the Baltimore Colts, saying he'd rather play baseball.

That was his fate after the 1983 draft and those were the words of a confident young man clearly in control of his destiny. The result was a $5 million signature for the Denver Broncos, who were eager to strengthen their offence after a unimpressive 2–7 record in the strike-shortened season.

Elway's signing-on bonus was $1 million and he took home a rookie's salary of $600,000. Great things were expected, the press and public watched every move.

The Denver newspapers and TV stations even ran regular 'Elway Watch' pieces devoted entirely to the headline-grabbing new boy.

Having entered the league in the same year as Miami's Dan Marino, Elway ended the season a firm second best and coach Dan Reeves admitted that in the euphoria of his arrival, he may have sent him into action before he was ready. The Stanford University star completed the 1983 season with the second to worst efficiency rating in the league and had twice as many interceptions as touchdowns.

With a year's NFL experience behind him, Elway led Denver to a divisional title in 1984 and in his third season set five new team passing records. He was named the Broncos' most valuable offensive player.

The following year he consolidated and grew in both confidence and maturity, before leading his team to a Super Bowl place at the end of the 1986 campaign.

Despite losing convincingly to the New York Giants, Elway threw for 304 yards with one touchdown and rushed for another. He had finally come out of Marino's shadow.

Elway had already been compared with the likes of Joe Nameth, Dan Fouts and Joe Montana. Coach Reeves says: 'If John doesn't have more talent than Joe (Montana), then he has at least as much.'

Elway's unique talent is scrambling. Anyone who watched Super Bowl XXI will recall how the evasive quarterback scurried free of the approaching Giant defense to make that extra yard for himself, even with a damaged and heavily strapped ankle. Marino has a different style altogether and comparing the two, Reeves said: 'Taking all Marino's accomplishments into consideration, I'd still take John. We need

someone able to run around, we couldn't have somebody like Marino just drop back there in the pocket.'

Despite all the praise, the vast sums of money, and his elevation to god-like status in Colorado, Elway remains as level-headed and humble as a man in his position can be.

He once stood cold and bruised outside his locker for 45 minutes talking to reporters, when they explained that they were in danger of missing their deadlines.

All the six-million-dollar man wanted was a hot shower, and who was to say he didn't deserve one.

1977 Ralston resigns as head coach (having given up his position as general manager the year before). He is replaced by Robert 'Red' Miller.
Western Division champions.

1978 AFC champions, defeating the Oakland Raiders.
Runners-up at Super Bowl XII, beaten by the Dallas Cowboys.

1981 The Broncos are bought by Edgar F. Kaiser Jr.

1983 In the most lucrative trade in NFL history, the Broncos sign quarterback John Elway to a five-year contract for $6 million — with the result that Elway becomes known as the 'six-million-dollar man'.

1984 Western Division champions.

1987 AFC champions, but lose to the New York Giants 39–20 in Super Bowl XXI.

★ ★ ★ ★ ★ ★ ★ ★ ★ ★ ★ ★ ★ ★ ★ ★

Detroit Lions

Pontiac Silverdome, 1200 Featherstone Road, Pontiac, Michigan 48057
(313) 335 4131

Stadium: Pontiac Silverdome. 80,638 capacity; AstroTurf.

Conference: NFC (Central Division)

Colours: Honolulu blue and silver

1934 Radio station owner George Richards buys the Portsmouth (Ohio) Spartans (who had entered the NFL in 1930) for $21,500, and moves them to Detroit. The winner of a contest on Richard's station renames them the Detroit Lions — to make the team 'the king of beasts' over the Detroit Tigers baseball team.

1935 NFL champions, defeating the New York Giants.

1938 The Lions move from the University of Detroit stadium to Briggs Stadium. Head coach Dutch Clark accuses owner Richards of 'meddling' in the possible transfer of a player from the Pittsburgh Steelers; the player is not transferred, and Clark leaves.

1939 The NFL fines Richards $5,000 for having given money to a potential player while he was still at college.
Richards sells the Lions to Chicago department store magnate Fred Mandel for $225,000.

1948 After owning the club for nine years — during which they ended five seasons near or at the bottom of the league (and one year, 1942, in which they won no games at all) — the disenchanted Mandel sells out to a syndicate of Detroit sportsmen and society people. End Bob Mann is hired as the team's first black player.

1949 The Lions finish fourth in the NFL, the first time since 1945 they have not been bottom of the league.

1950 The players revolt against head coach Alvin 'Bo' McMillin and he is dismissed with a $60,000 golden handshake to cover the remaining two years of his contract. The management vow never to sign contracts longer than one year with any further coaches.

1952 National Conference champions, defeating the Los Angeles Rams in a play-off.
NFL champions, defeating the Cleve-

land Browns — and ending the Lions' best season since 1934.

1953 NFL champions, again defeating the Cleveland Browns.

1954 Western Conference champions.

1957 Head coach Buddy Parker negotiates a two-year contract (having suffered under one-year contracts since 1950) and immediately announces, 'I can no longer control this team,' and resigns. His leaving may have been spurred by seeing his players socialising with the club's owners at a cocktail party — a practice he deplored.

1962 The Lions win the most games (11) in one season in the club's history, finishing second in the league.

1963 Star player, defensive tackle Alex Karras, and five other players, as well as the Lions' management, are fined by the NFL for betting on football games. Karras is also suspended for a minimum of one year.

1964 William Clay Ford of the motor car dynasty buys out all the other shareholders for $6.5 million to take control of the club.

1967 With the NFL's re-organisation, the Lions are placed in the Central Division of the Western Conference.
The Lions became the first NFL team to be beaten by an AFL team, in a pre-season inter-league game against the Denver Broncos.

1971 Wide receiver Chuck Hughes dies of a heart attack on the field during a game against the Chicago Bears.

1975 The Lions move to the Pontiac Metropolitan Stadium — later renamed the 'Silverdome' — the largest air-supported dome structure in the world.

1983 Central Division champions.

Hall of Fame members

Jack Christiansen: defensive back, 1951–8
Earl 'Dutch' Clark: back, 1931–2, 1934–8
Bill Dudley: back, 1947–9
Dick 'Night Train' Lane: cornerback, 1960–5
Yale Larry: defensive back/safety punter, 1952–3, 1956–64
Bobby Layne: quarterback/kicker, 1950–8
Ollie Matson: running back, 1963
Hugh McElhenny: running back, 1964
Joe Schmidt: linebacker, 1953–65
Doak Walker: 1950–5
Alex Woyciechowicz: centre, 1938–46

★ ★ ★ ★ ★ ★ ★ ★ ★ ★ ★ ★ ★ ★ ★ ★

Green Bay Packers

1265 Lombardi Avenue, Green Bay, Wisconsin 54307
(414) 494 2351

Stadia: Lambeau Field, PO Box 10628, 1265 Lombardi Avenue, Green Bay, Wisconsin 54307. 56,155 capacity; grass.
Milwaukee County Stadium, Highway I-94, Milwaukee, Wisconsin 53214. 55,958 capacity; grass.

Conference: NFC (Central Division)

Colours: dark green, gold and white

1919 Earl 'Curly' Lambeau persuades his employers, the Indian Packing Company, to provide $500 for equipment for a football team. The team takes its name from this association.

1921 The team joins the American Football Association.

The franchise for the team is awarded to John Clair of the Acme Packing Company, with Lambeau as star halfback, passer, publicity man, general manager and coach.

1922 Clair is ordered to return the franchise to the APFA because he had been paying players who were still at college. Curly Lambeau is awarded the franchise for $50.

Lambeau's tenure is in doubt: an insurance company refuses to pay out for a 'rain policy' when precipitation amounting to 0.09 of an inch stops a game, 0.01 of an inch less than that specified in the policy. When another game is washed out and there is no insurance, Lambeau almost gives up, but help is at hand in the form of Andrew Turnbull, publisher of the Green Bay *Press-Gazette*.

1923 Turnbull forms a group — the 'Hungry Five' — who cancel the Packers' debts and campaign for civic support. The community of Green Bay rise to the occasion, shares are sold and the Green Bay Football Corporation is born.

1929 During this unbeaten season — the first in the league since the Canton Bulldogs' in 1923, 20,000 fans surge on to the railway tracks in front of the train carrying the team (who had just defeated the Chicago Bears to win the NFL championship) and force the train to stop.

1930 The Packers' string of 22 wins and no defeats finally ends when they lose to the St Louis Cardinals.
NFL champions.

1931 NFL champions.

1933 When a fan falls out of the temporary stands at the Packers' stadium and sues, and then the team's insurance company fails, the Packers go into receivership. Once again, the 'Hungry Five' come to the rescue: a 'Save the Packers' fund is started, and Green Bay residents, from school children to businessmen, raise $15,000. The club is incorporated, with all profits to go to retired servicemen's organisations.

1936 NFL champions, defeating the Boston Redskins.

1938 Western Division champions.

1939 NFL champions, defeating the New York Giants.

1941 Western Division champions.

1944 The Packers field a team of untried newcomers, older players and servicemen on leave, to become NFL champions, defeating the New York Giants.

1947 Lambeau is criticised by the executive committee of the club for buying a training camp with land and cottages for coaching staff and their wives. Club management is reorganised into subcommittees.

1948 With the team winning fewer than half their games, Lambeau begins to fine each player half-a-week's salary for each loss.

1950 After 31 years with the club, Lambeau resigns amid a dispute with the citizen-owned club corporation. To make matters worse, the training camp burns down and attendances (and income) have hit bottom. New shares are sold to raise $125,000.

1957 The team moves into the new $1 million City Stadium.

Quarterback Randy Wright.

1958 The executive committee hires Ray 'Scooter' McLean as head coach. Players take advantage of his 'nice guy' manner, which leads to the worst season in Packers' history: 1 win, 10 defeats.

1959 Vince Lombardi, hired as head coach and general manager, on the first day of his eventual 10-year career with the club states: 'Let's get one thing straight: I'm in complete command here.' He spends three months watching films of the previous season's Packers games. By the end of the year, the team has had their best season since 1945: 7–5–0.

1960 Western Conference champions, after a win over the Los Angeles Rams highlighted by a 91-yard touchdown pass by quarterback Bart Starr.

1961 NFL champions, defeating the New York Giants. Running back/kicker Paul Hornung scores 19 points in that game.

1962 NFL champions, again defeating the New York Giants at Yankee Stadium in temperatures plummeting to 20°F with a 40 mph wind.

1963 NFL suspends Hornung, the team's top scorer, indefinitely for betting on the Packers and other teams.

1964 Hornung is back on the squad after his suspension but apparently has lost the ability to kick successfully under pressure.

1965 NFL champions, defeating the San Francisco 49ers by a field goal (kicked by Don Chandler) in the 14th minute of sudden death.

1966 City Stadium is renamed Lambeau Stadium in honour of the team's founder. NFL champions, defeating the Cleveland Browns.

1967 NFL champions, defeating the Dallas Cowboys on 2 January.
Champions of the first Super Bowl, defeating the Kansas City Chiefs.
NFL champions, defeating the Dallas Cowboys in arctic conditions (−13°F) at Green Bay on 31 December, in what came to be known as the 'Ice Game'.

1968 Champions of Super Bowl II, defeating the Oakland Raiders.
In a shock announcement, Vince Lombardi retires as coach; he stays on as general manager.

1969 Lombardi leaves the Packers for the Washington Redskins. (He dies of cancer the following year).

1970 The Packers tie for the last place in their division.

1971 New coach Dan Devine's leg is broken when he is run over on the sidelines by a New York Giant player during the first game of the season.

1972 Central Division champions. Bumper stickers appear carrying the slogan 'The Pack Is Back'.

1975 Former star player Bart Starr appointed head coach.

1984 Starr replaced by former team-mate Forrest Gregg.

Hall of Fame members

Herb Adderley: defensive back, 1961–9
Johnny Blood (né McNally): back, 1929–33, 1935–6
Tony Canadeo: back, 1941–3, 1946–52
Willie Davis: end, 1960–9
Forrest Gregg: tackle, 1956, 1958–70, coach, 1983–
Arnie Herber: back, 1931–41
Clarke Hinkle: back/kicker, 1932–41
Paul Hornung: half back/kicker

Cal Hubbard: tackle, 1929–35
Don Hutson: end/kicker, 1935–45
Walt Kiesling: tackle, 1935–6
Earl 'Curly' Lambeau: back, 1921–30, coach, 1919–49
Vince Lombardi: coach, 1959–68
Mike Michalske: guard, 1929–35, 1937
Ray Nitschke: linebacker, 1958–72
Jim Ringo: centre, 1953–63
Bart Starr: quarterback, 1956–71
Jim Taylor: back, 1958–66
Emlen Tunnell: back, 1959–61

Houston Oilers

(see also page 97)
Box 1516, Houston, Texas 77001
(713) 797 9111

Stadium: Astrodome, Loop 610, Kirby and Fannin Streets, Houston, Texas 77054. 50,452 capacity; AstroTurf.

Conference: AFC (Central Division)

Colours: scarlet, Columbia blue and white

1959 The team is founded by K. S. 'Bud' Adams Jr, a Houston oilman, who names them the 'Oilers' for 'sentimental and social reasons': 'You think I'd ever call them the "Aluminiums" or "Uraniums"?' Adams jokes.

1960 All-America halfback and Heisman Trophy winner Billy Cannon is signed

Running back Butch Woolfolk

(after a dispute with the Los Angeles Rams, for whom Cannon had also agreed to play), and veteran quarterback George Blanda is lured out of retirement.

Lou Rymkus is appointed head coach.

Adams leases Jeppesen High School stadium and spends $200,000 to renovate it and increase seating capacity to 36,000.

Eastern Division champions.

1961 The Oilers win the first AFL Championship, defeating the Los Angeles Chargers on New Year's Day.

After the Oilers win only one of their first five games, Rymkus is replaced by his assistant Wally Lemm. After the changes in coaches, the Oilers are victorious 10 times in a row and become the first professional team to score more than 500 points in one season.

AFL champions, defeating the San Diego Chargers.

1962 Lemm leaves to become coach of the St Louis Cardinals, and is replaced by Frank 'Pop' Ivy — the Oilers' third coach in three years.

Runners-up for the AFL championship, defeated by the Dallas Texans in an historic *six*-quarter, double-time game which ends 20–17.

1963 The Oilers suffer their first losing season: 6–8–0.

1964 Ivy is replaced by Sammy Baugh, who at the end of another losing season (4–10–0) is, in turn, replaced by Hugh 'Bones' Taylor. Baugh stays on to help his successor, and the Oilers' coach, Lou Rymkus, also returns as offensive line coach.

1965 Although the new Houston Astrodome is now complete, the team management announce that the Oilers will not play

there because of 'an unrealistic lease agreement', and sign a lease to play at the Rice University stadium instead.

1966 'Bones' Taylor is also unable to come up with the goods — he had a 4–10–0 season the previous year — and Wally Lemm returns as coach.

1967 Eastern division champions: with this success, the Oilers become the first team ever to go from the bottom of the league to the division championship in one season.

1968 The teams moves into the Astrodome after all.

1970 The Oilers, in one of the most emotional games in the AFL's history, defeat the Dallas Cowboys for the first time in a pre-season game.

1971 On Lemm's retirement, Ed Hughes is named head coach. However, during the dismal 4–9–1 season, during which both the offensive line and offensive backfield coaches are sacked, Hughes' contract is terminated 'by mutual consent'. He is replaced by Bill Peterson of Rice University.

1973 When the team under Peterson wins only one game in 19 outings, he is fired and replaced by the veteran Sid Gilman as head coach and general manager.

1974 The Oilers finish with seven wins and seven losses — their best record since 1969. However, the management announce a record loss of $459,281.

1975 O. A. 'Bum' Phillips is named head coach, but although Gilman wants to remain general manager, he is forced to give that up to Phillips as well.

The Oilers end the season with a 10–4–0 record, their first winning season since 1967. Houston home attendances reach an all-time high.

Mike Rozier

1979 Runners-up for the AFC Championship, defeated by the Pittsburgh Steelers.

1980 Runners-up for the AFC Championship, again defeated by the Pittsburgh Steelers.
After the Oilers are defeated in the play-offs by the eventual Super Bowl winners — this time, the Oakland Raiders — for the third time in a row, 'Bum' Phillips is relinquished as coach.

1981 Ed Biles becomes head coach.

1983 After the team winning only one game the previous year, Biles is relieved of duty after six games and is replaced by Chuck Studley, who only manages a 2–14–0 season.

1984 Studley is replaced by Hugh Campbell: the Oilers' record for the year stands at 3–13.

1985 With a second losing season under his belt (5–11), Campbell is released.

Hall of Fame members

George Blanda: quarterback/kicker, 1960–6
Ken Houston: safety, 1967–72

Indianapolis Colts

PO Box 5400, Indianapolis, Indiana 46254
(317) 252 2658

Stadium: Hoosier Dome, 100 South Capitol Avenue, Indianapolis, Indiana 46225. 60,127 capacity; AstroTurf.

Conference: AFC (Eastern Division)

Colours: royal blue, white and silver

1952 After the franchise in Baltimore folds (after being active 1946–50), the NFL faces a lawsuit by Baltimore shareholders unless it is reinstated. NFL Commissioner Bert Bell agrees that the Dallas Texans can transfer to Baltimore if 15,000 season tickets can be sold within six weeks. The target is met in 4½ weeks.

1953 With ticket sales resulting in $300,000 in the bank, Carroll D. Rosenbloom takes over as majority shareholder.
Keith Molesworth is named first head coach of the reconstituted team, which is now called the 'Colts' after the defunct Baltimore team.

1954 Molesworth becomes chief talent scout and is replaced by Wilbur C. 'Weeb' Ewbank. He promises to produce a championship team within five years.

1956 At the end of an erratic season, Ewbank's job is saved by a 53-yard scoring pass against the Washington Redskins by understudy quarterback Johnny Unitas, who had been signed that year.

1958 After winning five consecutive games, the Colts come up against the Green Bay Packers. This is a 56–0 shut-out, but it costs the team Unitas, who suffers broken ribs and a punctured lung.
After the team lose one and win one, Unitas returns, wearing a special harness to protect his ribs. The team goes on to win the Western Conference championship.
NFL champions, defeating the New York Giants. Trailing 17–14 with 8 seconds left on the clock, linebacker Steve Myrha kicks a 20-yard field goal to even the score and enter the two teams into sudden death overtime for the first time in league history. A pass from Unitas to fullback Alan Ameche enables the latter to score a touchdown and bring victory to the Colts, 23–17. A crowd of 30,000 fans meet the team at the airport on their return from New York.

1959 NFL champions, again defeating the New York Giants.

1960 Unitas suffers a cracked vertebra and, although he can pass well (his 47-game touchdown passing streak is only stopped by the Los Angeles Rams in mid-December), he is forbidden to run. With this and other team injuries, the Colts finish 6–6–0.

1963 Weeb Ewbank is replaced by Don Shula, who is only 33.

1964 Rosenbloom buys all the stock in the Colts that is held in other hands and becomes sole owner of the club.
Western Conference champions.

1965 With a team record of 9–1–1, both Unitas and number-two quarterback Gary Cuozzo are injured. Running back Tom Matte is transferred to the quarterback position and performs flawlessly, but the Colts are defeated in sudden death overtime in the Western Conference play-offs by the Green Bay Packers.

The Colts in their white away kit playing the Buffalo Bills in New York

1967 The Colts are transferred into the Coastal Division.

1968 NFL champions, defeating the Cleveland Browns to end the season with a ten-game winning streak.

1969 Super Bowl III runners-up, losing to the New York Jets (who are now coached by Weeb Ewbank, formerly of the Colts).
The Colts are moved into the new American Conference of the NFL.

1970 Despite protests by owner Rosenbloom, Shula moves to Miami to coach the Dolphins. This is the beginning of a long-standing feud between the two men.

1971 AFC champions, defeating the Oakland Raiders.
Super Bowl V champions, defeating the Dallas Cowboys 16–13
Winnetka, Illinois executive Robert Irsay gains control of the Colts: he first buys the Los Angeles Rams and then trades them with the Rosenblooms for the Colts.

1973 Unitas is transferred to the San Diego Chargers — the end of an era.

1975 Ted Marchibroda is named head coach: his appointment marks the fifth since Shula left in 1969.
Eastern Division champions.

1976 After the Colts lose four of its six pre-season games Irsay lashes out against both the team and coach Marchibroda. The latter resigns, but after the players issue a statement saying that Irsay and general manager Joe Thomas 'have completely destroyed this team', Marchibroda agrees to return with complete control over football matters. Eastern Division champions.

1977 Eastern Division champions.

1980 After two 5–11–0 seasons, Marchibroda is replaced by Mike McCormack.

1981 Team manages to win only two of its 16 games, McCormack is fired and Frank Kush, a Canadian Football League coach, takes over.

1983 After a miserable 0–8–1 season in 1982, the Colts have first pick of the collegiate draft. However, first choice John Elway states that he would rather play baseball than join the Colts (he eventually goes to the Denver Broncos for $6 million).

1984 The team is transferred to Indianapolis, where there are 143,000 season ticket requests in two weeks.

1985 The new Indianapolis Colts, now under coach Rod Dowhower, finish their second season in their new home with a 5–11–0 record.

1986 Rod Dowhower is sacked after the Colts crash to 0–13. Former Patriots coach Ron Mayer takes over to become the tenth Indianapolis coach in 14 years. Owners Robert and Harriet Irsay get divorced but stay faithful to their team. Robert watches from the directors' box, while his estranged wife takes her seat in the stand.

Hall of Fame members

Raymond Berry: end, 1955–67
George Blanda: quarterback, 1950
Art Donovan: defensive tackle, 1950, 1953–61
Weeb Ewbank: coach, 1954–62
Gino Marchetti: defensive end, 1953–64, 1966
Lenny Moore: running back, 1956–67
Jim Parker: tackle/guard, 1957–67
Joe Perry: running back, 1961–2
Y. A. Tittle: quarterback, 1948–50
Johnny Unitas: quarterback, 1956–72

✦ ✦ ✦ ✦ ✦ ✦ ✦ ✦ ✦ ✦ ✦ ✦ ✦ ✦ ✦ ✦

Kansas City Chiefs

1 Arrowhead Drive, Kansas City, Missouri 64129
(816) 924 9300

Stadium: Arrowhead Stadium (*address as above*). 78,094 capacity; AstroTurf 8.

Conference: AFC (Western Division)

Colours: red, gold and white

1959 Texas millionaire Lamar Hunt, unable to get an NFL franchise for his home city of Dallas, establishes and organises the American Football League and its six original teams, one of which is the Dallas Texans. (NB: this is a completely different team from the Dallas Texans which formed the basis of the Indianapolis Colts.) After the league is formed and the Texans are in place, the NFL establishes the Dallas Cowboys.
Hunt appoints as coach Hank Stram, a disciplinarian who is notable for having said: 'Show me a good loser, and I'll show you a loser — period.'

A name like Harvey Lee Yeary isn't really the sort of name dreams are made of. But conjure up the image of tv's *Six Million Dollar Man* think of a new name — Lee Majors — and you're on your way to fame. That was the road taken by Yeary and a highly successful one it's proved! Unfortunately, the graduate of Eastern Kentucky University who went on to play the part of Steve Austen didn't have the 'Six Million Dollar Man' body; a back injury brought his football career to an abrupt end.

1962 AFL champions, defeating the Houston Oilers.

1963 The mayor of Kansas City promises Hunt three times as many season ticket sales and the enlargement of the Municipal Stadium there if he will move the Texans to Kansas City. This Hunt does, also persuaded by the fact that the nearest professional football franchise is 250 miles away (whereas the Texans had been competing against the Dallas Cowboys and the Houston Oilers). He renames the team the 'Chiefs'.
The Chiefs arrive to ill omens as rookie Stone Johnson suffers a fatal injury in a pre-season game.

1964 The Chiefs play erratically during a season when ten regulars are injured, including tight end Fred Arbanas, who is mugged on a Kansas City street and blinded in one eye. With a 7–7–0 record, attendances fall.

1966 Following the Chiefs' first winning season in 1965, and intrigued by the signing of Heisman Trophy-winner, running back Mike Garrett for $400,000, attendances pick up dramatically, with 43,885 turning out to see the Chiefs lose to the Buffalo Bills at the season's opening game at home.
Western Division champions.

1967 AFL champions, defeating the Buffalo Bills. The Chiefs are mobbed at the airport in Kansas City on their return.
Runners-up of the first Super Bowl, losing to the Green Bay Packers.

1970 AFC champions, defeating the Oakland Raiders.
Super Bowl IV champions, defeating the Minnesota Vikings.
Relations between star running back Garrett and coach Stram become strained, and Garrett is traded to the San Diego Chargers. In the final game of the season, he is instrumental in the Chargers' defeat of the Chiefs.

1971 Western Division champions.

1972 The team moves into the new futuristic Arrowhead Stadium.

1974 The Chiefs have their first losing season since 1963: 5–9–0.

1975 Paul Wiggin of the San Francisco 49ers is appointed head coach.

1976 After losing six of their first seven games, Wiggin is fired and succeeded by Tom Bettis. The team dedicate their next game — against the Green Bay Packers — to Wiggin, and win. However, a six-game losing streak results in Bettis's contract not being renewed.

1981 The Chiefs, now with Marv Levy as coach, have their first winning season since 1973: 9–7–0.

1983 John Mackovic, formerly of the Dallas Cowboys, is appointed head coach.

1986 A wild card gives Kansas their first play-off spot for 15 years.

1987 John Mackovic is replaced as head coach by former special teams coach Frank 'Crash' Gansz, and must count himself as one of the unluckiest coaches in the NFL to be dismissed.

Hall of Fame members

Bobby Bell: linebacker
Lamar Hunt: owner, 1960–
Willie Lanier: linebacker
Len Dawson: quarterback

The Astrodome in Houston Texas, where the Houston Oilers play at home. Opened in 1965 at a cost of $38 million, it was the first indoor arena

Los Angeles Raiders

332 Center Street, El Segundo, California 90245
(213) 322 3451

Stadium: Los Angeles Memorial Coliseum, 3911 South Figueroa Street, Los Angeles, California 90037. 92,600 capacity; grass.

Conference: AFC (Western Division)

Colours: silver and black

1960 Following the withdrawal of the Minneapolis/St Paul franchise from the newly formed American Football League, Barron Hilton, owner of the Los Angeles Chargers, threatens to pull out too if another franchise is not given to a city on the West Coast. Oakland is that city, and the franchise becomes the property of a syndicate headed by Y. C. 'Chet' Soda.

The team is named the 'Raiders' and Eddie Erdelatz is appointed head coach.

When the University of California refuses permission for the team to use their stadium, the Raiders move into Kezar Stadium in San Francisco, which they share with NFL rivals, the 49ers.

1961 The Raiders move to Candlestick Park in San Francisco. Ed McGah, Robert Osborne and Wayne Valley buy out the other shareholders, and McGah is made president of the club.

After the Raiders lose their first two games in shut-outs — 55–0 against the Houston Oilers and 44–0 against the Chargers (who had by now moved to San Diego) — Erdelatz is fired after admitting 'I don't know what to do about it.'

Marty Feldman is named head coach, but his tenure sees the Raiders scoring the fewest and allowing the most points in the league, winning only two games in front of mostly empty seats.

1962 When co-owner Valley threatens Oakland city officials that the club will be moved unless a new stadium is built, the team is given Frank Youell Field, a high school stadium, which, when expanded to hold 20,000, still loses money even when every seat is filled.

Feldman is replaced with Bill 'Red' Conkright after two games, but the Raiders fail to win until the very last game of the season — ending a 13-game losing streak.

Mike Haynes

1963 After refusing several times, Al Davis of the San Diego Chargers agrees to replace the luckless Conkright and become head coach and general manager. He proceeds to reorganise both the management and the team sides of the franchise completely.

The Raiders have their first winning season since their formation — 10–4–0 — winning their last game, against the Houston Oilers, 52–49: the highest scoring game in AFL history.

1966 Davis leaves the Raiders to become AFL Commissioner, and is succeeded by John Rauch. However, when the AFL and NFL merge, Davis resigns and takes over as managing general partner of the Raiders.

The team moves into the new Oakland-Alameda County Coliseum.

1967 AFL champions, defeating the Houston Oilers.

1968 Runners-up at Super Bowl II, defeated by the Green Bay Packers.

One of the highlights of the 1968 season was what came to be known as the 'Heidi game'. The Raiders were trailing the New York Jets 32–39 when the tv network showing the game switched over to the film *Heidi* when there were still 65 seconds to play. Despite the fact that the switchboard at NBC was immediately swamped with angry protests, viewers were not allowed to see the two last-minute touchdowns by the Raiders which won them the game, 43–32.

Western Division champions.

1969 Rauch leaves to become head coach of the Buffalo Bills and is replaced by Raiders' assistant John Madden — at 32, the youngest head coach in professional football.

Western Division champions.

1970 The Raiders are the first AFC team to become Western Division champions four times in a row, largely thanks to the veteran 43-year-old quarterback/kicker George Blanda, who that season produced four victories and a tie in the final seconds of five consecutive games.

1972 Western Division champions.

1973 Western Division champions.

1974 Western Division champions.

1975 Western Division champions.

1976 George Blanda retires after a 15-year career in professional football.
Western Division champions: the Raiders' ninth divisional title in ten years.
AFC champions, defeating the Pittsburgh Steelers.

1977 Super Bowl XI champions, defeating the Minnesota Vikings.

1978 The Raiders miss the AFC play-offs for the first time since 1971 (they had taken part the year before in the wild card game).

1979 After 10 years of producing divisional victories and winning the Super Bowl, John Madden retires as head coach. Former Raiders' quarterback Tom Flores replaces him.

1980 The Raiders, with an 11–5–0 record, win a wild card spot in the AFC play-offs.

1981 AFC champions, defeating the San Diego Chargers.
Super Bowl XV champions, defeating the Philadelphia Eagles.
The Raiders' management, along with the Los Angeles Coliseum Commission, want the team to move into the Memorial Coliseum, the Los Angeles Rams having transferred to Anaheim Stadium but are blocked by the NFL. The Raiders and the Commission bring a lawsuit against

Ray Guy of the Raiders' special team performing his speciality — punting

the NFL monopoly, but this ends in a mistrial.

The Raiders have their first losing season — 7–9–0 — since 1964.

1982 In a retrial, the Raiders win the right to move to the Los Angeles Memorial Coliseum, which has the largest seating capacity of any football stadium in the US. In December, in a game between the Raiders and their rivals, the Los Angeles Rams, more than $1 million worth of tickets are sold — a first in the NFL. The Raiders win.

1984 AFC champions, defeating the Seattle Seahawks on New Year's Day.
Super Bowl XVIII champions, defeating the Washington Redskins.
The Raiders are awarded the key to the city of Los Angeles in recognition of their achievements.

1985 Western Division champions.

1986 The Raiders lose 0–37 to Seattle, their first shut-out since moving to LA in 1981.

Hall of Fame members

George Blanda: quarterback/kicker, 1967–75
Ron Mix: tackle, 1971
Jim Otto: center, 1960–74
Gene Upshaw: guard

Super Bowl — what could be a more famous competition name? — was coined in 1966 by Lamar Hunt, owner of the Kansas City Chiefs.

Los Angeles Rams

2327 West Lincoln Avenue, Anaheim, California 92801
(714) 535 7267 or (213) 585 5400

Stadium: Anaheim Stadium, 1900 State College Boulevard, Anaheim, California 92806. 69,007 capacity; grass.

Conference: NFC (Western Division)

Colours: royal blue, gold and white

1937 Team founded in Ohio as the Cleveland Rams. Owner Homer Marshman chooses their name because 'wild rams butt heads harder than any other animal' and also because he admires the Fordham University Rams.

1941 Team sold to Fred Levy Jr and Daniel F. Reeves, who at 29 becomes the youngest owner in professional football.

1943 Reeves becomes sole owner of the team. He obtains permission from the NFL to suspend operations for a year, because of the world war.

1945 NFL champions, defeating the Washington Redskins. Despite the Rams being league champions, the team attracts only 45,000 fans during the whole season and Reeves loses $50,000. He buys Los Angeles Memorial Coliseum in preparation for his bid for an LA franchise.

1946 Initially the other owners in the NFL refuse Reeves permission to move his franchise to Los Angeles, but when he

101

threatens to sell the Rams and get out of football altogether, they finally agree.

The Rams hire Kenny Washington and Woody Strode, the first black players in the NFL since 1933.

1947 Having fired general manager Chile Walsh, Reeves takes over that position. Increasing financial losses force him to take on partners; these receive 'one of the best bargains in sports history', one obtaining 30 per cent of the stock for one dollar and a share of the debts (15 years later, Reeves has to pay $4.8 million to buy them out). The losses were partly due to the fact that the Los Angeles Dons, the All-America Football Conference team, attracted far larger crowds.

1949 Western Division champions.

With the acquisition of a second quarterback, a controversy raged over which man was number one — an argument which continued (with a number of different personnel involved) for many years.

1950 The AAFC folds, and the Rams are the only team left in Los Angeles.

National Conference champions.

1951 NFL champions, defeating the Cleveland Browns. The Rams' backfield is now known as the 'Bull Elephants'.

1954 Rumours of dissent between coach Hampton Pool on the one hand and the coaching staff on the other seem proved as the Rams decline into fourth place and all the assistant coaches resign.

1955 Pool resigns. Reeves and the other owners then set out on a widely publicised hunt for a new coach, finally (and anti-climactically) appointing Sid Gillmann of the University of Cincinnati.

Western Conference champions.

After arguments among the owners, Reeves is relieved of his directorship of the club.

1957 Pete Rozelle is appointed general manager.

1959 After the Rams finish the season at the bottom of the Western Conference, Gillmann and his entire staff resign.

1960 Rozelle leaves to become NFL Commissioner; Reeves appoints former player Elroy 'Crazy Legs' Hirsch to replace him. Another former star, Bob Waterfield, is hired as head coach, and he brings along former coach Hampton Pool as an assistant.

1962 In an auction which involves celebrity Bob Hope and others, Reeves reacquires control of the franchise for $7.1 million. A new corporation — the Los Angeles Rams Football Company — is formed with Reeves owning 51 per cent of shares and the rest distributed between 11 minority shareholders.

1963 The recurring quarterback problem causes the team to lose their first five games, and it is only when Roman Gabriel is appointed number one quarterback that the Rams go on to win five of their last nine games. David 'Deacon' Jones, Merlin Olsen, Lamar Lundy and Roosevelt 'Rosey' Grier make an impact in the defensive front line, and become known as the 'Fearsome Four'.

1966 George Allen is appointed head coach.

1967 Coastal Division champions.

Nolan Cromwell, Rams' defense team strong safety

1968 Personal differences lead Reeves to fire coach Allen, resulting in an outcry from the team, many members of which appear at a televised press conference on his behalf.

1969 On New Year's Day Reeves asks Allen to return, but the latter takes six days to agree.

1970 At the end of the year it is announced that Allen's contract is not to be renewed. He has tied with Sid Gillmann for lasting the longest of any of the Rams' coaches — five years.

1971 Reeves dies of Hodgkins' disease.

1972 The Reeves estate sell the franchise to industrialist Robert Irsay for $19 million. He, in turn, trades it to Carroll Rosenbloom for the Baltimore Colts and $3.4 million.

1973 Western Division champions.

1974 Western Division champions. James Harris becomes the first black quarterback to lead a professional team to a championship.

1975 Western Division champions.

1976 Western Division champions.

1977 Western Division champions.

1978 When coach Chuck Knox resigns to go to the Buffalo Bills, George Allen returns. However, after two losses before the official season, he is 'released' and is succeeded by Ray Malavasi.
Western Division champions.

1979 Rosenbloom drowns while swimming off Florida coast; his wife Georgia (now Georgia Frontiere) becomes majority owner of the club.
Western Division champions.

1980 NFC champions, defeating Tampa Bay Buccaneers on 6 January.

1983 Western Division champions.

1984 Western Division champions.

1986 Eric Dickerson finishes the season with the most yards in the NFL (1,821) and also the most fumbles (11).
Wild card entry to the play-offs.

Hall of Fame members

Tom Fears: end, 1948–56
Bill George: linebacker, 1966
Elroy 'Crazy Legs' Hirsch: end/rightback, 1949–57, general manager, 1960–9
David 'Deacon' Jones: defensive end, 1961–71
Dick 'Night Train' Lane: defensive back, 1952–3
Ollie Matson: running back/end, 1959–62
Merlin Olsen: defensive tackle, 1962–76
Dan Reeves: team owner, 1941–71
Andy Robustelli: defensive end, 1951–5
Norm Van Brocklin: quarterback/punter, 1949–57
Bob Waterfield: quarterback/defensive back/kicker/punter, 1945–52

Tony Nathan, running back with the Dolphins

The Dolphins are the only team to have played a Super Bowl game without scoring a touchdown. In Super Bowl VI against the Dallas Cowboys the only score for the Dolphins was a 31-yard field goal.

Miami Dolphins

4770 Biscayne Boulevard, Suite 1440, Miami, Florida 33137

(305) 576 1000

Stadium: Orange Bowl, 1501 NW Third Street, Miami, Florida 33125. 75,206 capacity; grass.

Conference: AFC (Eastern Division)

Colours: aqua, coral and white

1965 Minneapolis attorney Joseph Robbie, while representing a friend in his bid for an AFL franchise for Philadelphia (he did not succeed), is persuaded by AFL Commissioner Joe Foss to apply for one for Miami. Robbie joins forces with entertainer Danny Thomas, and together they raise the $7.5 million for the franchise. Miami Mayor Robert King High agrees to invite the AFL to Miami after some behind-the-scenes advice from US Vice-President Hubert Humphrey, a friend of Robbie.

In a statewide 'name the team' contest, Mrs Robert Swanson of West Miami wins two lifetime passes for her entry (out of 20,000): 'Dolphins'. According to Mrs Swanson, 'The dolphin is intelligent and indigenous to this area.' Co-owner Robbie expands on this at the naming ceremony on 8 October: 'The dolphin is one of the fastest and smartest creatures of the sea. Dolphins can attack and kill a whale or a shark. Sailors say bad luck will come to anyone who harms a dolphin.'

1966 George Wilson, formerly of the Detroit Lions and the Washington Redskins, is named head coach.

Conditions for the team are, at first, rather less than perfect. They practise on a gravel-covered field; their dormitory is next door to Sea World and they are kept awake by the barking of the seals. Their first pre-season game against the San Diego Chargers follows a miserable 10-hour flight to California in a propeller-driven aeroplane: they lose, 30–10.

Although the Dolphins are defeated in their first regular game, against the Oakland Raiders, the 26,776 Florida fans thrill to the sight of running back Joe Auer (who is also notable for owning a pet lion) returning the opening kick-off 95 yards for a touchdown.

When quarterbacks Rick Norton and Dick Wood are injured, coach Wilson sends in his son George Jr, who leads the Dolphins to their first AFL victory, against the Denver Broncos.

1967 W. H. Keland of Racine, Wisconsin buys out three of the minority shareholders. Then Keland and Robbie buy out Danny Thomas.

1969 Robbie buys Keland's interest in the team to become the majority shareholder.

As the Dolphins plummet to last place, due to injuries to a large extent, George Wilson is fired.

1970 Don Shula, former coach of the Baltimore Colts, is named head coach and vice-president of the club. Shula says that 'The only way I know is hard work', and goes on to prove it with the team as they embark on a gruelling training camp schedule involving two-mile runs every morning at 7 o'clock, two daily

90-minute practices and an evening walk-through.

All the practice pays off as the Dolphins win four pre-season games running and have a four-game winning streak at the beginning of the regular season. They go on to win a wild card spot in the play-offs, finally losing to the Oakland Raiders.

1971 Eastern Division champions.
In the divisional play-offs the Dolphins defeat the Kansas City Chiefs 27–24 in the longest game in NFL history: 82 minutes, 40 seconds.

1972 AFC champions, defeating the Baltimore Colts.
Runners-up at Super Bowl VI, beaten by the Dallas Cowboys.
The Dolphins are the first team in NFL history to go unbeaten and untied all season, including post-season games.
With the Dolphins' 52–0 shut-out over the New England Patriots, Shula becomes the first coach to win 100 games in 10 seasons (with both the Baltimore Colts and the Dolphins).
AFC champions, defeating the Pittsburgh Steelers.

1973 Super Bowl VII champions, defeating the Washington Redskins.
The Dolphins' perfect record is broken with two defeats in the 1973 season, but this still leaves them with the best two-year record in NFL history: 26–2–0.
AFC champions, defeating the Oakland Raiders — the first time any team has won the championship three times in a row.

1974 Super Bowl VIII champions, defeating the Minnesota Vikings.
In a shock announcement, star players Larry Csonka, Jim Kiick (both running backs) and Paul Warfield (wide receiver) reveal they have signed a deal worth $3.3 million to play for the Toronto Northmen in the World Football League, and will be leaving the Dolphins in 1975. Eastern Division champions.
In the play-offs the Dolphins' domination of professional football ends when the Oakland Raiders win with a touchdown pass thrown in desperation in the last seconds of the game.

1976 Shula experiences his first losing season in 14 years as an NFL head coach when the Dolphins end the year with a 6–8–0 record.

1979 Eastern Division champions.

1980 A shoulder injury ends the career of quarterback Bob Griese, who has been with the team since their record season.

1981 Eastern Division champions.

1982 AFC champions, defeating the San Diego Chargers.

1983 Runners-up at Super Bowl XVII, beaten by the Washington Redksins.
In a first in Dolphin history, a quarterback — Dan Marino — is drafted, after 26 other NFL teams pass him up. He goes on to make 20 touchdown passes and becomes the first rookie quarterback ever voted to start in the Pro Bowl.

1984 Eastern Division and AFC champions.
Marino becomes the first NFL quarterback to pass for over 5,000 yards.

1985 Runners-up at Super Bowl XIX, defeated by the San Francisco 49ers.
Eastern Division champions.

Hall of Fame members

Larry Csonka: running back
Jim Langer: centre

Minnesota Vikings

9520 Viking Drive, Eden Prairie, Minnesota 55344
(612) 828 6500

Stadium: Hubert H. Humphrey Metrodome, 500 11th Avenue S, Minneapolis, Minnesota 55415. 62,212 capacity; SuperTurf.

Conference: NFC (Central Division)

Colours: purple, white and gold.

1960 Max Winter wins a franchise from the NFL to set up a team in Minnesota.

1961 General manager Bert Rose invents the team name 'Vikings' and the first team is formed, comprising mainly players past their prime, with Norm Van Brocklin, former quarterback with the Los

Injury forced Hall of Famer Jim Otto to retire — he'd suffered a broken nose ten times, a broken jaw, three left-knee operations and six right-knee operations.

One of the all-time greats, Fran Tarkenton, a 1986 Hall of Fame entrant, who played quarterback with the Vikings for 13 seasons and retired in 1978 holding NFL records in nearly every passing category

The Vikings in their white gear

Angeles Rams and the Philadelphia Eagles, as head coach. However, the draft results in the hiring of one Fran(cis) Tarkenton, an outstanding quarterback from the University of Georgia, who threw four touchdown passes as well as scoring himself in the Viking's first NFL game — a 37–13 upset over the Chicago Bears.

1964 Despite the Vikings becoming accepted as a full-blooded NFL team, Rose is replaced as general manager.
In a game with the San Francisco 49ers, defensive end Jim Marshall gains a place in the record books by picking up a fumble and carrying it 66 yards *the wrong way*, for a 49ers' safety. The Vikings still won, 27–22.

1965 When the Vikings fail to win the Western Conference title as expected, coach Van Brocklin announces he is resigning. He changes his mind the next day.

1966 Team morale reaches a low point, as relations between them and their coach continue to sour. In particular, Van Brocklin and Tarkenton are barely on speaking terms .

1967 Tarkenton issues a statement that either he goes or Van Brocklin does. In fact, both go: first Van Brocklin resigns; then, a month later, Tarkenton is traded to the New York Giants.
Harry 'Bud' Grant is appointed head coach.

1968 Central Division champions.

1969 Western Conference champions.

1970 NFC champions, defeating the Cleveland Browns in a freezing 8°F.
Runners-up at Super Bowl IV, losing to the Kansas City Chiefs.
Central Division champions. The Vikings' strength lies in their mighty defense: they allow only 14 touchdowns in 14 games during the regular season.

1971 Central Division champions.
Defensive tackle Alan Page named the most valuable player in the NFL.

1972 Fran Tarkenton returns to the Vikings and has an outstanding year, although the team itself finishes with a disappointing 7–7.

1973 NFC champions, defeating the Washington Redskins.

1974 Runners-up at Super Bowl VIII, losing to the Miami Dolphins.
NFC champions, defeating the Los Angeles Rams.

1975 Runners-up at Super Bowl IX, losing to the Pittsburgh Steelers.
Central Division champions.

1976 NFC champions, defeating the Los Angeles Rams.

1977 Runners-up at Super Bowl XI, losing to the Oakland Raiders.
Central Division champions.

1978 Central Division champions.

1979 Long-serving star Fran Tarkenton retires.
The team has its first losing season since 1967.

1980 Central Division champions.

1982 The team moves from Metropolitan Stadium to the new Humphrey

1986 Quarterback Tommy Kramer finishes the season as the league's leading quarterback, with a percentage rating of 92.6.

Hall of Fame members

Hugh McElhenny: running back, 1961–2
Fran Tarkenton: quarterback, 1961–7, 1972–9

iking linebacker Matt Blair

New England Patriots

Sullivan Stadium, Route 1, Foxboro, Massachusetts 02035
(617) 543 7911 *or* 262 1776

Stadium: Sullivan Stadium. 60,890 capacity; Super Turf.

Conference: AFC (Eastern Division)

Colours: red, white and blue

1959 The AFL's eighth franchise is awarded to Boston and William H. 'Billy' Sullivan Jr — the first time a professional football team has been established in the city since the demise of the Boston Yanks in 1949.

1960 Lou Saban of Western Illinois University is named head coach. He is described by the team's general manager, Ed McKeever, as 'a Paul Brown [of Cleveland Browns' fame] with heart'.
A Boston newspaper runs a contest to pick the team's name. 'Patriots' is the winner, submitted by 74 people in the light of Boston's position in the history of the American Revolution.
The team signs to play at Boston University's football field for at least two years. In April the Patriots become the first club to issue public stock. By the end of the year, the team has lost about $350,000.

1961 With the club managing to sell fewer than 3,500 season tickets, they enter the year on rocky financial ground. The situation is made worse as the team loses two of its first five games, and the fans stay away. Saban is fired, and Mike Holovak is named head coach. The

Patriots, now stressing defense, continue with a 7–1–1 record, and attendances increase to an average of more than 19,000 per game. Financial losses continue but not at the same perilous rate.

1963 The team move to Fenway Park, home of the Boston Red Sox baseball team. Eastern Division champions.

1964 At the end of a 10–3–1 season, the club announces that they have made profits for the first time.

1969 After two consecutive losing seasons, Holovak is replaced by Clive Rush — who proceeds to lose the first seven games of the season.
All home games are now played at Boston College Alumni Stadium.

1970 Joe Kapp is transferred from the Minnesota Vikings for a large sum, but by the end of the year the out-of-condition quarterback has made only three touchdown passes and 17 interceptions.
By mid-season, coach Rush is fired and replaced by John Mazur, but the Patriots still end the year with a dismal 2–12–0 record.
After failing to find financing for a projected $80 million stadium in central Boston, the club selects Foxboro, Massachusetts — about 35 miles southwest of Boston — as the team's future home. In the meantime the Patriots play at home at Harvard Stadium.

1971 Because of the move out of Boston the team's name is changed to the 'New England Patriots'.
The new Schaefer Stadium at Foxboro (so named because the Schaefer brewing company bought $1 million worth of Patriots' stock) is inaugurated by a preseason win over the New York Giants.

1972 Mazur and general manager Upton Bell

The New England Patriots 1985 season's players, coaches, equipment managers, president . . . among others!

feud over plans to build up the team.

Quarterback Jim Plunkett, rookie star of the previous year, is subjected to massive physical punishment by a leaky offensive line, and the defense is notable for its inexperience as several veteran players are transferred.

The Mazur/Bell feud is resolved when the head coach resigns before the end of the season and Bell is fired soon after.

1973 Chuck Fairbanks of the University of Oklahoma is hired as head coach and general manager.

1975 With Plunkett frequently out of action through injury, Fairbanks begins to depend more and more on his number two quarterback, Steve Grogan. When Plunkett returns to health, there is con-

troversy over which quarterback is the best.

Club president Sullivan buys additional voting stock to become majority shareholder with 83 per cent of the franchise.

1976 Plunkett is traded to the San Francisco 49ers and Grogan reigns supreme.

With an 11–3–0 record, the Patriots have their best season ever, winning a wild card spot in the play-offs, only to be defeated by the Oakland Raiders, the eventual Super Bowl champions, in the last 39 seconds of the game.

1978 Eastern Division champions.

Shortly after Fairbanks announces that he is resigning to return to collegiate coaching at the University of Colorado, the Patriots lose their final game of the regular season to the Miami Dolphins.

The team loses the divisional play-off game against the Houston Oilers.

1979 Ron Erhardt, former Patriots' assistant, is named head coach.

1981 Following a 10–6–0 season in 1980, the Patriots collapse, ending with the worst record (2–14–0) in the NFL. Erhardt is fired at the end of the season.

1982 Ron Meyer of Southern Methodist University is named the new head coach.

1983 The Patriots make it to the play-offs for the first time since 1978 but lose to the Miami Dolphins.
Schaefer Stadium is officially renamed 'Sullivan Stadium' in honour of the team's owner.

1984 Raymond Berry replaces Ron Meyer as coach in mid-season, four days after the Patriots lose 44–24 to the Miami Dolphins and the day after Meyer fires popular defensive co-ordinator Rod Rust. Rust is given his job back.

1985 Eastern Division and AFC champions.

1986 Runners-up at Super Bowl XX, defeated by the Chicago Bears.
There are shocking revelations that some members of the team are involved with drugs.
Eastern Division champions.

Hall of Fame member

Raymond Berry: coach, 1984–

New Orleans Saints

1500 Poydras Street, New Orleans, Louisiana 70112
(504) 522 1500

Stadium: Louisiana Superdome (*address as above*). 71,684 capacity; AstroTurf.

Conference: NFC (Western Division)

Colours: old gold, black and white

1966 The NFL grant a franchise to New Orleans. Millionaire racing-car buff John W. Mecom Jr becomes majority shareholder. One of his partners is jazz trumpeter Al Hirt.

1967 Team named the 'Saints' after the Dixieland classic (and one of Hirt's favourite numbers) 'When the Saints Go Marching In'.
The Saints play their first game at Tulane University stadium against the Los Angeles Rams in front of 80,789 fans (20,000 of whom had bought season tickets the day the box office opened). Despite rookie John Gilliam returning the opening kick-off 94 yards for a touchdown the team loses.

1970 In the first game helmed by new coach J. D. Roberts, the Saints upset the Detroit Lions. The two-point lead is scored in a 63-yard field goal by Tom Dempsey, a free-agent kicker born with no toes on his right foot and with no right hand.

1972 Former astronaut Richard F. Gordon Jr is appointed executive vice-president of the club. Despite the assistance of the man who had piloted Apollo XII to the

The Louisiana Superdome, largest indoor stadium on earth

Richard Todd (now retired)

1981 O. A. 'Bum' Phillips is named head coach.

1983 The Saints equal their best season (1979): 8 wins and 8 defeats.

1984 Owner John Mecom Jr puts the Saints on the market for $75 million. They are bought for $70 million by Tom Benson.

1985 'Bum' Phillips retires. He is replaced as head coach by his son Wade Phillips.

1986 Veteran defensive lineman Derland Moore is released after 14 years' service. He played a record 169 games and outlasted five head coaches.

Hall of Fame members

Doug Atkins: defensive end, 1967–9
Jim Taylor: running back, 1967

moon and back, the Saints equal their worst-ever season: 2–11–1.

1975 The team moves into the Louisiana Superdome, the world's largest indoor stadium.

1976 Hank Stram is appointed head coach — the fifth since the team was formed ten years before. (He lasts only two years.)

1980 The Saints finish a disastrous season, winning only once and losing 15 times. Coach Dick Nolan (after the standard two years) is fired the day after the 12th loss.

New York Giants

Giants Stadium, East Rutherford, New Jersey 07073
(201) 935 8111

Stadium: Giants Stadium. 76,891 capacity; AstroTurf.

Conference: NFC (Eastern Division)

Colours: blue, red and white

1925 Timothy J. Mara purchases an NFL franchise for $2,500 (he had intended to buy an interest in champion boxer Gene Tunney). He names his team the 'Giants' after the baseball team whose stadium — the Polo Grounds — they will share.

The New York Giants' 1985 season line-up

With the assistance of 5,000 free tickets, 25,000 attend to watch the Giants' first game on their home ground; they lose to the Frankford (Pennsylvania) Yellow-jackets. Despite winning the next seven in a row, the team fail to pull in the crowds until the Chicago Bears — with star player Red Grange — come to town: 70,000 turn out to watch and Mara suddenly finds that owning a pro football team is financially rewarding.

1926 Mara and his Giants find themselves fighting for audiences with the rival New York Yankees, an AFL team also named after a local baseball club. Mara hits back by issuing free tickets and providing entertainment and games between school teams before each Giants game, but by the end of the season, he has lost $40,000. However, the Yankees lose 2½ times that and the AFL folds.

1927 The NFL ensures that the Yankees play only when their games will not conflict with those of the Giants.
NFL champions.

1930 Tim Mara's two sons, Wellington and Jack, take over ownership of the club.

At the end of a season which saw them second only to the Green Bay Packers, the Giants play a charity game against Knute Rockne's Notre Dame All-Stars, winning 21–0 and raising $115,153 (an astronomical sum for the time) for the New York Unemployed Fund.

1933 Eastern Division champions.

1934 NFL champions, defeating the Chicago Bears. This contest became known as the 'Sneakers Game', after the Giants' equipment manager made a quick trip to Manhattan College and returned with basketball shoes (i.e. 'sneakers') for some of the Giants' players to give them more grip on the icy turf.

Only once has a wild card team won the Super Bowl. Advancing from the regular season with an 11–5 record, the Los Angeles Raiders won four post-season games on the trot. Super Bowl victory was theirs when they beat Philadelphia in Super Bowl XV.

New York would not have had the Giants without its founder Tim Mara, who weathered severe financial losses to turn the team into a major one. A deserving original member of the Hall of Fame

1935 Eastern Division champions.

1938 NFL champions, defeating the Green Bay Packers.

1939 Eastern Division champions.

1941 Eastern Division champions.

1944 Eastern Division champions.

1946 Eastern Division champions.
Just before the NFL championship game against the Chicago Bears (which the Giants lost), quarterback Frank Filchock and Merle Hapes are both questioned about an attempt by a New York bookmaker to fix the game. Filchock is immediately suspended for

not reporting the contact, but Hapes is allowed to play.
Both are subsequently suspended indefinitely.

1949 New York now has three pro football teams: the Giants and the Bulldogs, both NFL and both sharing the Polo Grounds; and the Yankees, a new All-America Football Conference team founded in 1946.

1952 Frank Gifford (later an ABC-TV football commentator) joins the team as a defensive back.
The Giants' fortunes dip dramatically, with Steve Owen, coach since 1931, still employing A and T formations.

1954 Jim Lee Howell is appointed head coach. In turn, he hires the young Vince Lombardi as his offensive coach.

1956 The Giants sign a contract to play at Yankee Stadium.
NFL champions, defeating the Chicago Bears.

1958 Runners-up for NFL championship, losing to the Baltimore Colts.

1959 Founder Tim Mara dies.
Vince Lombardi leaves to become head coach of the Green Bay Packers.
Eastern Conference champions.

1961 Eastern Conference champions.

1962 Eastern Conference champions.

1963 Eastern Conference champions, with quarterback Y. A. Tittle having his best year, including 36 touchdown passes.

1965 Club co-owner Jack Mara dies; his responsibilities are taken over by his brother Wellington.

1967 The Giants obtain quarterback Fran Tarkenton from the Minnesota Vikings, but the trade uses up most of the team's draft choices and leads to a lack of new players the following year.

1973 The Giants play their last game at Yankee Stadium, finishing off the season at the Yale Bowl in New Haven, Connecticut, preparatory to moving to the new Giants Stadium.

1975 As the new stadium is not yet completed, the Giants are forced to share Shea Stadium with the New York Jets, their games having to be scheduled for Saturday afternoons so that they do not conflict with the Jets'.

1976 The Giants finally move into Giants Stadium in East Rutherford, New Jersey. They lose to the Dallas Cowboys in their first game there, the fifth in a nine-game losing streak; after the seventh, head coach Bill Arnsparger is sacked.

1980 After a brilliant start with a victory over the St Louis Cardinals, the team fall to eight defeats in a row, prompted by a deluge of injuries which left 35 players out of action.

1981 The Giants defeat the Philadelphia Eagles in the wild card game for the divisional championship. (They are later defeated by the San Francisco 49ers for the championship itself.)

1984 In play-offs, but lose to eventual Super Bowl champions San Francisco 49ers.

1985 Saw play-offs again. Quarterback Phil Simms finishes third of top ten quarterbacks.

1986 Best season in Giants' 62-year history, finishing as Eastern Division champions for the first time in 23 years, with a record of 14–2.

1987 Super Bowl XXI champions beating the Denver Broncos 39–20 at Pasadena.

Hall of Fame members

Morris 'Red' Badgro: end, 1930–5
Roosevelt 'Rosey' Brown: tackle, 1953–65
Ray Flaherty: end, 1928–35
Frank Gifford: back/end, 1952–60, 1962–4
Joe Guyon: back, 1927
Mel Hein: centre, 1931–45
Wilbur 'Pete' Henry: tackle, 1927
Arnie Herber: back, 1944–5
Cal Hubbard: tackle, 1927–9, 1936
Sam Huff: linebacker, 1956–63
Alphonse 'Tuffy' Leemans: back, 1936–43
Vince Lombardi: offensive coach, 1954–9
Tim Mara: owner, 1925–59
Hugh McElhenny: back, 1963
Steve Owen: tackle, 1926–36
Andy Robustelli: defensive end, 1956–64
Ken Strong: back, 1933–5, 1939, 1943–7
Fran Tarkenton: quarterback, 1948–58
Jim Thorpe: back, 1925
Y. A. Tittle: quarterback, 1961–4
Emlen Tunnell: defensive back, 1948–58
Arnie Weinmeister: defensive tackle, 1950–3

✦ ✦ ✦ ✦ ✦ ✦ ✦ ✦ ✦ ✦ ✦ ✦ ✦ ✦

New York Jets

598 Madison Avenue, New York, New York 10022

(212) 421 6600

Stadium: Giants Stadium, East Rutherford, New Jersey 07073. 76,891 capacity; AstroTurf.

Conference: AFC (Eastern Division)

Colours: Kelly green and white

1959 New York City and Harry Wismer are awarded an AFL franchise.
The team is named the 'Titans', with blue and gold as team colours.

Sammy Baugh, former Redskins' quarterback, is hired as head coach at the (then) astronomical annual salary of $28,000.

1960 Wismer leases the Polo Grounds for the Titans' home games. He also signs a five-year deal to have the Jets' games televised: their fee for the first year is $1,785,000.

In their first game of the regular season the team draws an audience of just 9,607, of which 3,880 get in on free tickets.

1962 After two seasons with records of 7–7–0 Clyde 'Bulldog' Turner replaces Baugh, after Wismer agrees to pay off the remainder of Baugh's contract.

Wismer cannot meet the club's costs from its revenue and the AFL agree to assume the team's running costs until the end of the season.

1963 A five-man syndicate — comprising David 'Sonny' Werblin, Townsend B. Martin, Leon Hess, Donald Lillis and Phil Iselin — buy the Titans from Wismer for $1 million.

After the team's first losing season the year before Turner is let go and Weeb Ewbank is appointed the new head coach by the new owners. At the same time they change the team's name to the 'Jets'.

Attendances improve with the newly revitalised club.

1964 The team move to Shea Stadium, where 45,665 watch them defeat the Denver Broncos and, later, 60,300 are dismayed to see them beaten by the Buffalo Bills. The club trades draft rights so that they can pick University of Alabama quarterback Joe Namath — perhaps the most significant deal in the history of the NFL.

1965 Namath signs a Jets' contract worth $427,000. His start with the team is delayed by a knee operation but he is well enough by mid-September to play against the Kansas City Chiefs. In his first outing for a full game (in the Jets' loss to the Buffalo Bills) he throws for 287 yards.

By the end of the season Namath is twice named rookie of the year: he has gained 2,220 yards and has thrown 18 touchdown passes.

1966 Namath is responsible for the Jets' trouncing of the New England Patriots 38–28, ending the latter's hopes for the Eastern Division championship. Less than two weeks later he is back in hospital again, for further knee surgery.

1967 The Jets have their very first winning season: 8–5–1. Namath finishes the season having thrown for 4,007 yards — a record that stood for many years. His performance results in every home game being a sell-out.

1968 Sonny Werblin is bought out by his partners, and later in the year, Don Lillis dies.

One of the highlights of the Jets' best-ever season is the '*Heidi* game', when NBC TV show the beginning of a children's film rather than the final few minutes of the contest between the Jets and the Oakland Raiders: the Raiders score twice in the final 42 seconds to win. The television network's switchboard is inundated with protest calls from irate football fans.

AFL champions, defeating the Oakland Raiders.

1969 Namath 'guarantees' in an interview with sports reporters that the Jets will win Super Bowl III — a claim that helps to make the quarterback a legend.

Super Bowl III champions, defeating the Baltimore Colts. The Jets are the first

Mark Gastineau, defensive end, in action

Running back Freeman McNeill

AFL team to win the championship, and Ewbank is the first coach to have won it in both leagues.
Eastern Division champions.

1970 The Jets reverse their record, from 10–4–0 the year before to 4–10–0 this year, largely due to Namath's absence after a Baltimore Colts game in October because of a fractured right wrist.

1971 Running back John Riggins from the University of Kansas is signed up.

1972 Namath signs a contract for $250,000 a year, making him the highest paid player in professional football.

1973 In his last season before his retirement, Ewbank is joined by Charley Winner as an assistant for one year; Winner will succeed as coach in 1974.

1975 Namath turns down a multi-million-dollar offer from the new World Football League and signs a two-year contract with the Jets.
After the team loses seven out of nine games (including six consecutive losses), Winner is fired.

1976 Lou Holtz of North Carolina State University is named head coach.
The Jets match the previous year's losing record: 3–11–0. Despite his relatively new five-year contract, Holtz resigns to return to collegiate football before the end of the season.

1977 Walt Michaels, the Jets' defensive coach, is promoted to head coach.
Jim Kensil is named club president and chief operating officer.
Namath leaves the Jets and signs as a free agent with the Los Angeles Rams: it is the end of an era. He announces his retirement from professional football eight months later.

Again, the team ends the year with a 3–11–0 record.

1978 The Jets adopt a new logo and a new uniform.

1981 Leon Hess acquires more of the club until he is now owner of 75 per cent of the team.
The Jets have their first winning season (10–5–1) since 1969 and land a wild card spot in the play-offs, where they are defeated by the Buffalo Bills.

1983 Joe Walton, Jets' offensive co-ordinator and quarterback coach, takes over as head coach.

1984 The team leaves Shea Stadium for Giants Stadium in New Jersey, which they share with the NFC team.

1986 New team record of nine straight wins as Jets soar to 10–1. However, the winning run comes to an abrupt end with a 45–3 defeat by the Dolphins, the Jets' worst since 1979. They become the first team in NFL history to make the playoffs despite losing their last five games. Ken O'Brien breaks Joe Nameth's record of 15 straight completions.

Hall of Fame members

Weeb Ewbank: coach, 1963–73
Don Maynard: wide receiver

Aggression on the pitch is rife enough, but Mike Curtis (Baltimore Colts) was so wild he was even thrown out of practice sessions for fighting with his own team mates.

Philadelphia Eagles

Veterans Stadium, Broad Street and Pattison Avenue, Philadelphia, Pennsylvania 19148 (215) 463 2500

Stadium: Veterans Stadium. 73,484 capacity; AstroTurf.

Conference: NFC (Eastern Division)

Colours: Kelly green, white and silver

1933 Bert Bell and Lud Wray buy the franchise for the Frankford Yellowjackets and move it from the Philadelphia suburbs to the city proper, when a state law banning sports on Sunday is about to be repealed. Bell renames the team after the eagle which is the symbol of President Franklin Roosevelt's National Recovery Administration (established to deal with the effects of the Great Depression). The Eagles lose 56–0 in their first game, against the New York Giants, but then go on to win four in a row.

1935 Bell proposes instituting a 'draft', with the weakest clubs getting first pick of each year's graduating college players. The Eagles win only two games despite the efforts of halfback Alabama Pitts, who learned to play while serving time at Sing Sing prison.

1936 After the Eagles have lost $80,000, Bell buys out his partners for $4,000 and takes over as coach from Wray. The first draft is held, and Bell has first pick as coach of the lowliest team.
The team moves from the Baker Bowl to the Municipal Stadium.

1939 Bell signs Davey O'Brien, a 5-foot 7-inch quarterback, for $12,000 plus a percentage of the gate. He also has him insured by Lloyds of London, with the policy having to pay out $1,500 for every game O'Brien misses through injury; the money never has to be paid.

1940 The Eagles move from the Municipal Stadium to Shibe Park in North Philadelphia.
O'Brien retires to join the FBI.

1941 The Eagles have a new owner in Alexis Thompson of New York.
New coach Earle 'Greasy' Neale makes the most of his star quarterback Tommy Thompson — who, despite being blind in one eye, is a deadly long passer.

1942 The Eagles are one of the few NFL teams not to lose their quarterback to war service, since Thompson is rejected by the army because of his 'disability'.

1943 Because of squad losses due to the military call-up, and subsequent financial troubles, the Eagles and the Pittsburgh Steelers join forces. The result: the 'Phil-Pitt Steagles'.

1944 After a surprisingly successful year, the 'Steagles' separate.
Steve Van Buren of Louisiana State University, a halfback, is taken on during the college draft, and proves to be the making of the Eagles.

1947 Runners-up in the NFL championship, losing to the Chicago Cardinals. The Eagles are banned from wearing cleated shoes after being discovered sharpening their cleats to gain better traction on the slippery ground. Van Buren, in flat-soled shoes, slips and slides and gains only 26 yards in 18 carries.

'Greasy' Neale's 'Eagle' defense is overwhelmingly successful: a 5–2–4 alignment which is extremely physical and intimidating.

1948 NFL champions, defeating the Chicago Cardinals 7–0 in heavy snow. This might not have happened since the scorer of the game's only touchdown, Van Buren, had woken to discover the snow and, presuming that the game would be called off, went back to sleep; it was only after a frantic phone call from coach Neale that Van Buren raced to a trolley and reached the stadium in time to score.

1949 Alexis Thompson sells the franchise to a syndicate of 100 businessmen headed by James P. Clark for $250,000.
NFL champions, defeating the Los Angeles Rams in a game which saw the field turned into a muddy bog by heavy rain.

1950 The Eagles' fortunes begin to decline. Coach 'Greasy' Neale and owner Clark start a feud which has its climax in the locker room at the Giants' Polo Grounds, where the two have to be physically separated; Neale is fired at the end of the season.

1951 Alvin 'Bo' McMillin is hired as head coach but has to resign due to ill health after just two games. Wayne Millner succeeds him.

1952 'Bo' McMillin dies of stomach cancer, and Van Buren suffers the serious knee injury that forces him to retire.
Coach Millner is fired, and Jim Trimble replaces him.

1956 After a losing season, Trimble is usurped by Hugh Devore as head coach, but the latter is left with the weakest team in the Eastern Division as the Eagles' veteran line retires.

1958 Devore, too, is relieved of duty, and this time Buck Shaw is taken on as head coach. One of the first acts is to sign on the 32-year-old Norm Van Brocklin from the Los Angeles Rams — a decision that has much to do with the upturn in the Eagles' fortunes.
The Eagles move to the University of Pennsylvania's Franklin Field; attendances double.

1959 Bert Bell, former Eagles' owner and now NFL commissioner, suffers a fatal heart attack while watching the Eagles beat the Pittsburgh Steelers.

1960 NFL champions, defeating the Green Bay Packers. After the game, both coach Shaw and Norm Van Brocklin retire.

1961 Van Brocklin is outraged when Shaw's former assistant Nick Skorich is appointed head coach instead of him. He refuses to stay on as player-coach and leaves to become head coach of the Minnesota Vikings.
Sonny Jurgenson, the remaining and relatively untried quarterback, surprises everyone and proves to be one of the best players the Eagles have ever had, setting two league records and tying a third in his first season in the big time.

1962 Chairman of the board and former president James P. Clark dies.

1963 Quarterback Jurgenson and his back-up King Hill dramatically leave training camp to try to force management to increase their money. They do and the two players return.
Jerry Wolman, a building tycoon, buys the franchise for $5.5 million.

1964 Wolman hires as head coach and general manager Joe Kuharich, who promptly trades most of the Eagles' previous stars — e.g. Jurgenson and Tommy McDonald.

1966 Kuharich trades off more popular players, but the team ends up with its first winning season in five years.

1968 After the Eagles lose their first 11 games, fans begin to hope that they will remain winless and thus be able to nab college All-American O. J. Simpson in the draft; unfortunately (?), the team wins two of its last three games and the Buffalo Bills qualify for Simpson. Fans, disillusioned with Kuharich, start a 'Joe Must Go' campaign, complete with buttons as well as a skywriter over Franklin Field. Meanwhile, Wolman is fighting bankruptcy.

1969 Wolman is forced to sell the franchise to haulage magnate Leonard Tose of Norristown, Pennsylvania for $16.1 million. Tose fires Kuharich, and replaces him as general manager with former player Pete Retzlaff; Retzlaff himself hires another former player Jerry Williams as head coach.

1971 The Eagles move to Veterans Stadium. After two losing seasons and the beginning of another which saw three defeats in as many games, Tose fires Williams who, with the players' support, denounces the owner as 'a man of little character'. Williams' replacement, Ed Khayat, a fan of General George Patton, orders all the players to cut their hair and shave off their moustaches — an order that several team members, led by linebacker Tom Rossovich who was the star player the previous season, resist before acceding.

1972 Khayat's strict discipline and punishing contact drills result in three players being seriously injured during training camp.

Safety Lee Bradley and Rossovich jointly refuse to sign their contracts in a power struggle with general manager Retzlaff; Rossovich is traded and Bradley finally signs.

The morning following the Eagles' staggering 62–10 defeat by the New York Giants, Tose accepts Retzlaff's resignation and then fires the entire coaching staff.

1973 Mike McCormack is appointed head coach. One of his first acts is to sign on veteran quarterback Roman Gabriel from the Los Angeles Rams.

1975 After the favourites, the Eagles, fail to win over the Giants and Bears, coach McCormack states that he has 'two dogs' on his squad — a statement which angers his whole team. McCormack's contract is not renewed at the end of the season.

1976 Dick Vermeil becomes head coach — the fifth in nine years.

1978 The Eagles have their best season since 1960, finally reaching the play-offs (they lose to the Atlanta Falcons).

1979 The Eagles again reach the play-offs but are defeated by the Tampa Bay Buccaneers.

1980 NFC East champions.

It's not just car engines which need anti-freeze — pro football helmets need it too. Inside today's highly sophisticated polycarbonate, alloy, vinyl-foam, styrene and leather helmets, is a honeycomb of pods filled with liquid and anti-freeze. Their job — to absorb and distribute shocks to the head.

1981 NFC champions, defeating the Dallas Cowboys.
Runners-up at Super Bowl XV, losing to the Oakland Raiders.

1985 Coach Marion Campbell fired.

Hall of Fame members

Chuck Bednarik: centre/linebacker, 1949–62
Bert Bell: team owner, 1933–40
Bill Hewitt: end, 1936–9, 1943
Ollie Matson: back, 1964–6
Earle 'Greasy' Neale: head coach, 1941–50
Pete Pihos: end, 1947–55
Jim Ringo: centre, 1964–7
Norm Van Brocklin: quarterback, 1958–60
Steve Van Buren: back, 1944–51
Alex Wojciechowicz: centre/linebacker, 1946–50

 *Football's Loss . . .*

A reserve player for Whittier College, Richard Nixon was described by coach Wallace Newman as 'Although sometimes taking a lacing in scrimmage, he always came back for more'. Thirty-five years later he was President of the USA; it's interesting to consider if coach Newman would still stand by his summing up of Nixon. . .

In his autobiography Confessions of a Dirty Ballplayer Johnny Sample (Baltimore Colts) described himself as 'the baddest of them all'. A sample of his tactics was throwing the ball into the faces of opposing coaches.

Pittsburgh Steelers

Three Rivers Stadium, 300 Stadium Circle, Pittsburgh, Pennsylvania 15212
(412) 323 1200

Stadium: Three Rivers Stadium. 59,000 capacity; AstroTurf.

Conference: AFC (Central Division)

Colours: black and gold

1933 Former boxer and semi-pro football player Art Rooney Sr buys an NFL franchise for Pittsburgh for $2,500, naming the team the 'Pirates' after the hometown professional baseball team.
When Rooney comes up against state laws forbidding sporting events on Sunday, he solves the problem by giving free box seats at Forbes Field to the superintendent of police.
The team's first head coach is Forrest 'Jap' Douds.

1934 After a disappointing 3–6–2 season the previous year, Rooney replaces Douds with Luby DiMelio as head coach.

1935 DiMelio obviously doesn't have the winning touch either — the 1934 season ended with the Pirates at the bottom of the league for the second year running — so Rooney tries his third coach in three years, Joe Bach of Duquesne University.

1936 The Pirates have their best season yet. However, with only one game to win to clinch the divisional title, they are

Louis Lipps, Steelers' punt returner

forced to travel by train all the way to California to play an exhibition game for a friend of Rooney's, then travel all the way to the East Coast to meet the Boston Redskins. Exhausted, the Pirates lose in a 30–0 shut-out.

1937   Bach returns to college coaching and Rooney hires Johnny Blood (*né* McNally) — who had been a member of the team in 1934 but did not play because of injury — as player-coach. At 32, Blood (who took his name from the Rudolph Valentino film *Blood and Sand*) is irresponsible and unreliable. However, his extraordinary behaviour is offset by some stunning football: in his first game against the Philadelphia Eagles, he returns the opening kick-off to score a touchdown. This inspires the rest of the team.

1938   Rooney hires Byron 'Whizzer' White for $15,800 — the most money paid for a player at the time. White agrees to play only after postponing his acceptance of a Rhodes' scholarship.

By mid-season, the Pirates are in contention for the divisional title, but unbeknown to Blood, Rooney sells quarterback Frank Filchock and the team's offense crumbles.

1939   'Whizzer' White leaves for Oxford University; in his absence, Rooney sells the rights to him to the Detroit Lions.

After a 32–0 shut-out against the Chicago Bears, Blood packs his bags and walks out.

Walt Kiesling, Blood's assistant as well as a former Pirates' guard, takes over as head coach: he enforces curfews and

makes bed checks just to make sure. Despite this, the team ends the year 1–9–1.

1940   Rooney decides to change the team's image and their name: a contest results in the winning name 'the Steelers' — a reference to Pittsburgh's important steel industry.

The altered name makes no difference: the new Steelers end the season with a 2–7–2 record. Rooney is so disappointed that he sells the franchise to Alexis Thompson, a Philadelphia resident.

1941   Rooney buys an interest in the Philadelphia Eagles, but when he and Thompson discover they are both homesick for their respective hometowns, they swap franchises.

Bert Bell, who had been involved in Rooney's Philadelphia deal, takes over as the Steeler's head coach, but leaves after they lose two games. He is replaced by Buff Donelli, who tries to coach both the Steelers and the Duquesne University team at the same time. Eventually AFL Commissioner Elmer Layden rules that Donelli's dual coaching interests are inappropriate and Walt Kiesling again takes over.

1942   The Steelers have their first winning season (7–4–0), thanks to rookie halfback 'Bullet' Bill Dudley, who despite physical shortcomings wins through on sheer will power.

1943   The world war takes away many of the Steelers' players, so the team is merged with the Philadelphia Eagles to form the 'Phil-Pitt Steagles'.

1944   After having a creditable 5–4–1 season in tandem with the Eagles, the Steelers leave them to join the less effective Chicago Cardinals to form the 'Card-

The Steelers at a line of scrimmage

Pitts'. They are so bad that they become known as the 'Carpets: the team everybody walks on'.

After the third loss, three players are fined for 'indifferent play'. One is fullback Johnny Grigas, one of the few decent players; he becomes so disgusted with the team that he walks out minutes before the last game of the season — a 49–7 defeat by the Chicago Bears.

1945 The Steelers are back in Pittsburgh with Jim Leonard as head coach, but the team wins only two games all season, even though Dudley rejoins after military service.

1946 Leonard is replaced by Dr John B. 'Jock' Sutherland, a former winning college coach and a strict disciplinarian.

Dudley and Sutherland dislike each other on sight, but this does not affect the former's performance on the field. However, when Sutherland forces the halfback to play four games with injured ribs, Dudley tells Rooney that he will leave football unless the owner trades him at the end of the season. Rooney reluctantly lets him go to the Detroit Lions.

1947 With their first winning season since 1942, the team ties for the Eastern Division championship with the Philadelphia Eagles. Just before the play-off game, the players go on a one-day strike, demanding to be paid extra for an extra week's practice. This outrages Sutherland, and the upset tears the club apart: the Eagles win 21–0.

1948 Sutherland dies of a stroke and is replaced by his assistant John Michelosen. He, too, believes in strict discipline, but lacks Sutherland's ability. The Steelers begin to lose, ending the season 4–8–0.

1949 The team has a winning season (barely) — 6–5–1 — despite the fact that Michelosen retains single-wing formation, at a time when all other NFL teams have gone over to the T-formation.

1951 In his fourth year as coach Michelosen still uses the single-wing formation: this means that the Steelers rarely score, although they also allow few touchdowns because of their strong defensive line. Fans are bored and want to see a throwing game, particularly from Jim Finks, who Michelosen refuses to move from defense.

In the final game of the season Michelosen is forced to put Finks in the offense due to injuries sustained by other players. Finks lives up to his promise by completing 13 out of 20 passes to defeat the Washington Redskins 20–10, and Michelosen is fired a few days later.

1952 Rooney woos back Joe Bach as coach. Bach installs the T-formation and makes Finks a quarterback, and after taking time to adjust to the new regime, the team begins to win.

1954 Bach resigns due to illness and Walt Kiesling takes over for the third time. The Steelers do well, but after a battering contest with (and win over) the Philadelphia Eagles, the two teams are so knocked about that they both win only four of their next 14 games.

1955 The Steelers fall to last place for the first time since 1945.

1956 Quarterback Finks retires.

Pete (Fats) Henry, an original Hall of Fame member, who played for the Canton Bulldogs in the 1920s and was the largest player of his day

1957 Kiesling is replaced by Buddy Parker, former head coach of the Detroit Lions.

1958 Parker signs up quarterback Bobby Layne, who had played for him with the Detroit Lions. Layne is instrumental in producing a 7–4–1 winning season — the team's best since 1947.

1962 After two seasons plagued by injuries, Layne makes a startling comeback and leads the Steelers to their best-ever record: 9–5–0, finishing second in the Eastern Conference, with a wild card spot in the play-offs, which they lose to the Miami Dolphins.

1963 Layne retires, and tackle Gene 'Big Daddy' Lipscomb (acquired from the Baltimore Colts in 1961) dies of an apparent drugs overdose.
After a good start, the Steelers lose to the St Louis Cardinals after a 13-point lead. After coach Parker shrieks at them, 'You disgraced me, you disgraced yourselves,' the team win all but one of their next eight games, although usually only by the smallest of margins.

1965 After a 1964 season in which the Steelers fell to sixth place with a record of 5–9–0, coach Parker walks out just before the opening game, saying, 'I can't win with this bunch of stiffs.'
Under interim coach Mike Nixon, the Steelers have their worst season since 1945, winning only two of 14 games.

1966 Bill Austin is signed as head coach. He had been a line coach under Vince Lombardi at Green Bay, and with verbal abuse and battering practice sessions, he follows Lombardi's style. However, like Michelosen before him, he lacks his mentor's ability, and grumbling increases among the team members.

1968 A poor 2–11–1 season was notable for the 'O. J. game' against the Philadelphia Eagles. The Steelers, Eagles and the Buffalo Bills were all 'fighting' to have the poorest record so that they could have first pick of the college draft and thus obtain the miraculous Heisman Trophy-winning running back O. J. Simpson. The Steelers won against the Eagles and so lost Simpson (he eventually went to the Bills).
Bill Austin is fired at the end of the season.

1969 Chuck Noll, a former Baltimore Colts assistant, is hired as head coach.

1970 The Steelers are one of three NFL teams to be transferred to the American Football Conference following the merger of the NFL and AFL.
Because of the team's previous dismal record the year before (1–13–0), they have first pick of the college draft and choose quarterback Terry Bradshaw, who single handedly seems to raise the spirits of the team.
The Steelers move to their new home, Three Rivers Stadium.

1972 Rookie fullback Franco Harris joins the team and, in partnership with Bradshaw, lifts the team to their first winning season since 1963 and their best-ever record so far: 11–3–0.
Central Division champions — the first division title in the Steelers' 39-year history.
In the first of the play-offs, against the Oakland Raiders, Bradshaw and (particularly) Harris prove their worth. On their own 40-yard line, after a fourth-and-ten, the Steelers were behind 7–6 with 22 seconds left on the clock. Following three unsuccessful passes, Bradshaw tried one more time, aiming at John 'Frenchy' Fuqua; it missed him, bounced off the Raiders' Jack Tatum and

was caught by Harris in full stride, who took the 60-yard pass across the goal line to make the winning touchdown. This play came to be called the 'immaculate reception'. The Steelers went on to be defeated by the Miami Dolphins in the AFC championship game.

1973 Despite many players sidelined because of injuries — including Bradshaw, Harris and Fuqua — the Steelers end the year with a 10–4–0 record and a wild card spot in the play-offs.

1974 AFC champions, defeating the Oakland Raiders.

1975 Super Bowl IX champions, defeating the Minnesota Vikings.
In the regular season, after a 1–1 start the Steelers go on to win 11 in a row, showing their now awesome offensive and defensive power. In fact, the defense is now called the 'steel curtain'. A player of note is running back Rocky Bleier.
Central Division champions.

1976 AFC champions, again defeating the Oakland Raiders.
Super Bowl X champions, defeating the Dallas Cowboys. Despite hugging last place for the first eight weeks of the regular season, the Steelers then win ten straight (including five shut-outs) to gain their fourth Central Division title since 1972.

1977 After breaking his wrist early in October, Bradshaw comes back in a plaster cast to lead the team to its fifth Central Division championship title.

1978 Central Division champions.

1979 AFC champions, defeating the Houston Oilers.
Super Bowl XIII champions, defeating the Dallas Cowboys — the first team in the NFL to win the Super Bowl three times.
Central Division champions.

1980 AFC champions, again defeating the Houston Oilers.
Super Bowl XIV champions, defeating the Los Angeles Rams — the only team to have won it four times, and twice consecutively.
Because of injuries — including to the all-important Bradshaw — the Steelers' record falls to 9–7–0, and they miss the play-offs for the first time since 1971.

1982 Central Division champions.

1983 Bradshaw and Harris retire — the former as the Steelers' all-time leading passer, and the latter as the team's all-time leading rusher.
Central Division champions.

1984 Central Division champions.

1985 The Steelers have their first losing season — 7–9–0 — since 1971.

1986 Coach Chuck Noll takes his personal record against the New York Jets to 9–0 with a 45–24 victory. His career total goes to 170 wins.

Hall of Fame members

Bert Bell: owner, 1941–6
Johnny Blood (McNally): halfback, 1934, 1937–8, coach 1937–9
Bill Dudley: halfback, 1942, 1945–6
Cal Hubbard: tackle, 1936
Walt Kiesling: guard, 1937–8, coach, 1939–40, 1941–4, 1954–6
Bobby Layne: quarterback, 1958–62
Marion Motley: running back, 1955
Art Rooney Sr: owner, 1933–
Ernie Stautner: defensive tackle, 1950–63
'Mean' Joe Greene: defensive tackle

St Louis Cardinals

Busch Stadium, Box 888, St Louis, Missouri 63188
(314) 421 0777

Stadium: Busch Stadium, 200 Stadium Plaza, St Louis, Missouri 63102. 51,392 capacity; AstroTurf.

Conference: NFC (Eastern Division)

Colours: cardinal red, black and white

1899 Painter-decorator Chris O'Brien forms a neighbourhood team in Chicago's South Side.

1901 The team moves to a new field on a corner of Racine Avenue. O'Brien buys second-hand, faded maroon jerseys from the University of Chicago, the colour of which O'Brien dubs 'cardinal'. The team is now named the Racine Cardinals.

1906 Lack of competition forces O'Brien to disband the team.

1913 O'Brien re-forms the team and hires a coach; by 1917, they are champions of the Chicago Football League.

1918 After disbandment during the First World War and a subsequent flu pandemic, O'Brien forms the team for the third and last time.

1920 The Racine Cardinals become a charter member of the American Professional Football Association, the forerunner of the NFL.
John 'Paddy' Driscoll joins the team for $3,000 a year; an outstanding all-round athlete, he is probably the best drop-kicker of all time. He scores the only touchdown in a game with the Chicago Tigers — the winner of which (the Cardinals) would remain the only team to represent Chicago, the other one going out of business.

1921 Driscoll becomes player-coach.
For unknown reasons, O'Brien agrees that the Decatur Staleys (later to become the Chicago Bears) can move to Chicago — where they will compete for fans.

1922 The team changes its name to the 'Chicago Cardinals', and move to White Sox Park (where the eponymous baseball team plays).

1923 Quarterback Arnold Horween takes over as player-coach. A Harvard graduate and member of a wealthy family, Horween often takes to the field under the alias of McMahon and only occasionally takes money for playing.

1925 NFL champions.

1926 Under financial pressure, O'Brien is forced to sell Paddy Driscoll to the Chicago Bears for $3,500. In addition, the new American Football League's Chicago team, the Bulls, take a lease on the Cardinals' field; the latter are forced to move to the smaller Normal Field, which can hold fewer spectators, but without Driscoll, fewer people come anyway.

1929 After three losing seasons, O'Brien sells the team to a Chicago doctor, David Jones, for $25,000.
Jones moves the team to Comiskey Park and brings Ernie Nevers out of retirement to be player-coach. Nevers responds by scoring 40 points in six touchdowns and two field goals against the Chicago Bears.

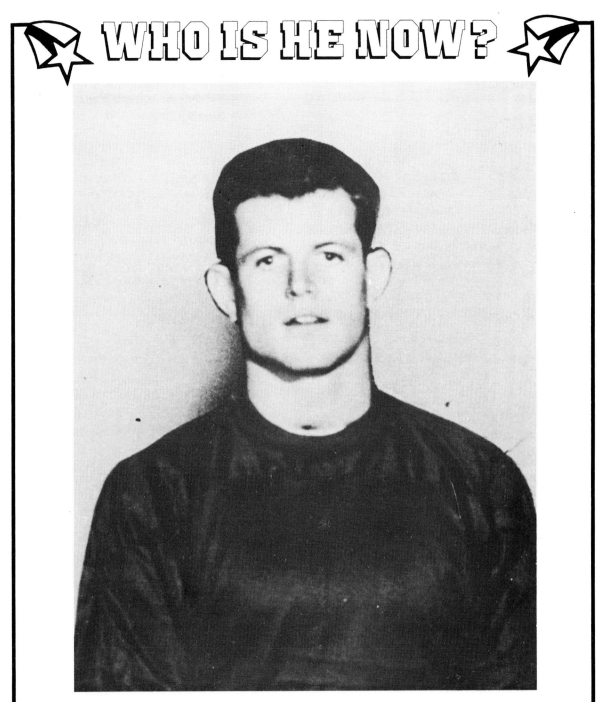

Edward M. (Ted) Kennedy played in 14 games for Harvard University during the 1954 and 1955 seasons. His success on the pitch was matched by his success as politician. Voted to the United States Senate in 1962, he's been re-elected ever since.

1930 The Cardinals play a charity game against the Bears (with proceeds going to unemployment relief) in the indoor Chicago Stadium — only 80 yards long. Earth is brought in to make a playing surface 6 inches deep.

1932 Ernie Nevers retires.
After three years of seeing the Cardinals on a downward slide, a chance remark during dinner on a yacht owned by Chicago magnate Charles W. Bidwell Sr leads to Dr Jones offering to sell the team to Bidwell, who is vice-president of the Chicago Bears. The asking price: $50,000 — twice what Jones had paid for it in 1929. Bidwell rids himself of his Bears' holdings.

1941 For the first time since 1937, the Cardinals do not finish last, even though they win only three games.

1942 The world war takes a heavy toll of the squad, with most of the best players going into the armed forces.

1944 Because of the lack of players, the Cardinals join forces with the Pittsburgh Steelers to form the 'Card-Pitts'. They fail to win any games.

1945 The Card-Pitts dissolve back into their previous forms.

1946 With the advent of the new All-America Football Conference and the birth of its Chicago team, the Rockets, Bidwell resolves to back his own team strongly, acquiring an outstanding set of rookies and hiring Jimmy Conzelman (coach between 1940 and 1942) for a second term.

1947 Bidwell hires Charley Trippi, the Georgia All-American halfback, for a then record $100,000 spread over four years. Trippi forms part of what Bidwell calls 'my million-dollar backfield'.

Charles Bidwell dies. His widow Violet authorises Ray Bennigsen to carry on. Wearing tennis shoes to counteract the frosty ground, the Cardinals become NFL champions, defeating the Philadelphia Eagles.

1948 After the Cardinals lose to the Philadelphia Eagles for the NFL championship on a snow-covered field, Conzelman resigns.

1949 Violet Bidwell marries Walter Wolfner, a St Louis executive; together they become involved in team management.

1950 Earl 'Curly' Lambeau, former coach of the Green Bay Packers, is hired as coach by Bennigsen, who resigns shortly after.

1951 Violet Bidwell Wolfner becomes chairman of the board; her sons Charles Jr ('Stormy') and Bill are named president and vice-president respectively. However, it is Walter Wolfner, now managing director, who has control. He quarrels with Lambeau for most of the season, until the latter resigns.

1955 With Ray Richards as coach, the Cardinals have their best season since 1950: 4–7–1. Highlight of the year is a devastating win over arch rivals, the Bears — 53–14.

1960 The Cardinals are moved to St Louis by the NFL to prevent the American Football League establishing a team there. They must share Busch Stadium with the Cardinals baseball team, and have nowhere to practise, having to settle for a city park.

1961 Violet Bidwell Wolfner dies, bequeathing 90 per cent ownership of the Cardinals (10 per cent had been sold to brewery tycoon Joseph Griesedieck) — to her two sons. Walter Wolfner contests the will, but it is declared valid. 'Stormy' and Bill Bidwell retain their previous titles, but begin to take much more active roles in team management.

1963 With a record of 9–5, the Cardinals have their best season since 1948, finishing third in the Eastern Conference.

1964 The Bidwells are approached by an Atlanta, Georgia syndicate with a view to moving the team to that city where a new stadium is almost ready (the new St Louis stadium was far behind schedule). When better terms are offered by the St Louis stadium authority and there is evidence of increased public support for the team, the Bidwells reject the Atlanta proposal.

1966 The Cardinals move into the new Busch Memorial Stadium.

1972 Bill Bidwell buys out his brother Charles' ('Stormy') share of the team.

1973 Bill Bidwell names Don Coryell as the Cardinal's 26th head coach.

1974 Eastern Division champions.
In the NFC divisional play-offs — the first time the team had been involved in any post-season competition since 1948 — the Cardinals lose to the Minnesota Vikings.

1975 Eastern Division champions.

1978 When coach Coryell resigns after the Cardinals fail to make the play-offs for two years running, veteran university coach Bud Wilkinson is appointed.

1979 Despite a losing season for the Cardinals, Ottis Anderson has the greatest season of any rookie running back in NFL history: he rushes for 1,605 yards and has nine 100-yard games — both league records.
Wilkinson is fired as head coach.

1980 Jim Hanifan is hired as coach.

1982 Eastern Division champions.

1985 With a dismal 5–11 record, key players on the injury list and plummeting morale, Bill Bidwell fires Jim Hanifan and his entire staff.
With the appearance of evidence of a drugs problem among some of his players, Bidwell contemplates moving the franchise to Phoenix.

Hall of Fame members

Charles W. Bidwell Sr: team owner, 1933–47
Guy Chamberlin: centre, 1927
Jimmy Conzelman: coach, 1940–2, 1946–8
John 'Paddy' Driscoll: back, 1920–5
Walt Kiesling: guard, 1929–33
Earl 'Curly' Lambeau: coach, 1950–1
Dick 'Night Train' Lane: cornerback, 1954–9
Ollie Matson: running back, 1952–8
Ernie Nevers: back/kicker, 1929–31
Jim Thorpe: halfback, 1928
Charley Trippi: halfback, 1947–55
Larry Wilson: safety, 1960–72

How to survive as a spectator . . .
Northern U.S. in the winter is cold, cold, cold, so learn from the experts — the players. Most of the following are pressed into service for use on the sidelines: women's tights; thermal underwear — tested for the Vikings by a party of Everest climbers; electrically heated benches — guess which part is kept warm!; and hairspray — not to keep the players looking pretty, but to act as a water repellant on shoes.

San Diego Chargers

San Diego Jack Murphy Stadium, PO Box 20666,
San Diego, California 92120
(619) 280 2111

Stadium: San Diego Jack Murphy Stadium, 9449
Friars Road, San Diego, California 92120. 60,100
capacity; grass.

Conference: AFC (Western Division)

Colours: blue, gold and white

1959   A Los Angeles team is one of the original six franchises of the newly formed American Football League. Barron Hilton (of the hotel chain) becomes owner of the team, which is to play at the Los Angeles Memorial Stadium.

Gerald Courtney of Hollywood wins a holiday to Acapulco for entering the winner of the 'name of the team' contest: he bases his entry — 'The Chargers' — on the battle cry of the University of Southern California football team: 'Cha-a-a-rge!'

1960   Sid Gillman, former coach of the Los Angeles Rams, is signed as head coach and, later, general manager. The player chosen to model the team's new uniform (blue and gold with lighting bolts on the helmet) is quarterback Jack Kemp, who

Charlie Joiner, Chargers' wide receiver (now retired)

138

Tight end Eric Sievers

as Senator Kemp of California is being groomed for the 1988 US presidential election.

At the start, audiences are sparse: the first game of the regular season (a 27–7 win over the New York Titans) is played in front of only 27,778 people — filling only about 30 per cent of the massive Coliseum's seats.

Western Division champions: the championship game against the Denver Broncos is watched by a crowd of only 9,928.

1961 Hilton reveals that he has lost almost $1 million in the Chargers' first season.

The city of San Diego, aiming to persuade Hilton to move his team there, increase ticket sales and enthusiasm for the Chargers among its citizens. The ploy works, and Hilton agrees. With permission from the AFL, the team moves into its new home, the enlarged (to 34,000 seats) Balboa Stadium.

With August temperatures soaring to 94°F, the Chargers defeat the Houston Oilers in their pre-season debut in San Diego.

Western Division champions.

1962 With Kemp (suffering from an injured throwing hand) traded to the Buffalo Bills for $100 and 23 players on the injury list for two or more games — and despite the signing of rookies Lance Alworth and John Hadl, wide receiver and quarterback respectively — the Chargers decline to a 4–10–0 season record.

1963 Barron Hilton and his father Conrad sell one-third of their interest in the team to a consortium of San Diego and Los Angeles business executives.

After training camp in the desert, the Chargers emerge at the end of the season with a winning 11–3–0 record. Western Division champions.

1964 NFL champions, defeating the Boston Patriots in the first week of January. Western Division champions.

1965 Star back Keith Lincoln and linebacker Frank Buncom hold out for more money, but eventually sign with the club. Defensive end Earl Faison and 22½-stone defensive tackle Ernie Ladd both announce that they will be working out their options: Ladd is fined, suspended and then finally reinstated.

Western Division champions.

1966 A syndicate of 21 businessmen, led by Eugene Klein and Sam Schulman of Beverly Hills, buy the Chargers for $10 million. Klein becomes president of the club (as well as co-general partner with Schulman) in place of Barron Hilton, but the latter — with his father — hang on to a substantial part of the club. They are joined as minority shareholders by George Pernicano, a restaurateur, and James Copley, publisher of a San Diego newspaper.

Despite signing a new five-year contract, coach Gillman is unable to lift the team from a 7–6–1 record: the first time they have not won the Western Division title since their establishment.

1967 The team move into the new San Diego Jack Murphy Stadium — Jack Murphy was the sports editor of the *San Diego Union* newspaper. In the pre-season inaugural game the Chargers meet their first NFL opponents, being defeated by the Detroit Lions.

1969 The Chargers have their biggest crowd yet — 54,042 — attracted by the chance to see Joe Namath and the New York Jets in action; despite Broadway Joe's presence, the Chargers win.

Gillman announces his retirement as coach, due to ill health; he will continue as general manager. The Chargers' offensive backfield coach Charlie Waller succeeds him.

1970 The team has its first losing season — 5–6–3 — since 1962.
At the end of the year Gillman returns as head coach and Waller goes back to offensive backfield duties.

1971 Club president Eugene Klein announces Gillman's retirement 'by mutual consent'. Harland Svare, a former Los Angeles Rams coach who had already taken over as general manager, is now also appointed head coach.

1973 After two further losing seasons, Svare announces the signing of the Baltimore Colt's star quarterback Johnny Unitas, who is now 40 years old. However, after only three games, an old back injury is aggravated during a contest with the Pittsburgh Steelers and Unitas is rendered virtually motionless. He spends most of the rest of the year on the bench, and retires from professional football in July of the following year. When Unitas is injured, rookie quarterback Dan Fouts takes over.
Svare resigns as head coach, staying on as general manager.

1974 Tommy Prothro, also a former LA Rams coach, is hired as head coach.
Training camp is interrupted by veteran players picketing as part of an NFL Players' Association dispute.

1975 The Chargers have their worst season ever: 2–12–0.

1976 Svare is fired as general manager and replaced by Johnny Sanders.
In the first NFL game outside the United States, the Chargers are defeated by the St Louis Cardinals in Tokyo in August. The team's record — 6–8–0 — is,

although a losing one, their best since 1971.

1977 Quarterback Fouts retires for 125 days, then returns to play in the last four games.

1978 After a disappointing 1–3 start, Prothro resigns and is succeeded by Don Coryell, formerly of the St Louis Cardinals, as head coach.
The Chargers have their first winning season — 9–7–0 — since 1969, helped by Dan Fouts' 24 touchdown passes.

1979 With their best record for 16 years (12–4–0), the Chargers become Western Division champions for the first time since 1965.

1980 Western Division champions.

1981 A holdout during a contract dispute leads to the trading of star wide receiver John Jefferson to the Green Bay Packers. Western Division champions, achieved with the aid of Dan Fout's spectacular 4,802-yard passing record.

1984 Wide receiver Charlie Joiner sets an NFL record with his 650th pass reception. The mayor of San Diego proclaims 11 December 'Charlie Joiner Day'.

1986 Joiner breaks Don Maynard's record for receiving yardage when he takes his total to 11,843 in the game against Seattle.
Don Coryell resigns and is replaced by London born Al Saunders.

1987 Charlie Joiner retires, but stays on as receivers' coach.

Hall of Fame members

Lance Alworth: wide receiver, 1962–70
David 'Deacon' Jones: defensive end, 1972–3
Ron Mix: tackle, 1960–9
Johnny Unitas: quarterback, 1973

San Francisco 49ers

711 Nevada Street, Redwood City, California
94061
(415) 365 3420

Stadium: Candlestick Park, San Francisco,
California 94124. 61,185 capacity; grass.

Conference: NFC (Western Division)

Colours: 49er gold and scarlet

1946 Anthony J. 'Tony' Morabito, partner in
Lumber Terminals of San Francisco,
forms a team that is a charter member of
the new All-America Football Conference (having been refused an NFL
franchise). E. J. Turre and Allen E.
Sorrell, both partners of Morabito, are
both credited with giving the team its
name, a reference to the prospectors
who flocked to California following the
discovery of gold in 1849.

1947 Morabito — a 'nut with a hearing aid in
San Francisco', according to a
Washington Redskins broadcaster —
buys out his partners for $100,000 and
splits ownership of the team 75/25 per
cent with his brother Vic.

1949 The 49ers enter the NFL.

1951 Quarterback Y. A. Tittle is acquired
from the defunct Baltimore Colts
franchise.

1952 Tony Morabito suffers a heart attack.
Rookie Hugh McElhenny, a halfback,
has a spectacular first season.

1953 After their best season since they joined
the NFL, losing only three games,

Morabito gives fullback Joe Perry a
bonus cheque for $5,090 — $5 for each
of the 1,018 yards he had rushed.

1954 The 49ers now have one of the best
backfields in pro football history, with
fullback John Henry Johnson from the
Pittsburgh Steelers joining Tittle,
McElhenny and Perry.

1955 Buck Shaw, the team's first and only
coach, is fired after nine years with the
49ers. His replacement is Norman 'Red'
Strader, who is unpopular for his strict
discipline.

1956 Strader is replaced by Frankie Albert, a
former 49ers' quarterback.

1957 Tittle and rookie end R. C. Owens
(standing 6 feet 5 inches tall) invent the
'Alley-Oop' pass: Tittle throws the ball in
a high arc, and Owens outjumps any
opponents to catch it.
Trailing the Chicago Bears 17–7 at half-
time, coach Albert tells the team that
owner Tony Morabito, aged only 47, has
suffered a fatal heart attack; the team
rally to make an emotional comeback
and win 21–17.

1958 Vic Morabito takes over the team's
operation.

1960 Coach Howard 'Red' Hickey (who had
succeeded Frankie Albert in 1959
institutes the 'shotgun' formation: the
quarterback, standing 3–5 yards back,
takes a long snap from the centre, then
passes or hands off. Using this, the 49ers
win four of their last five games.

1961 After an appalling loss to the Chicago
Bears, Hickey abandons the shotgun
formation and returns to the T formation;
he says, however, that he would have
continued with the shotgun if his players
had not lost confidence in it.

1962 The 49ers have their first losing season since 1956: six wins and eight losses.

1963 Hickey resigns and is replaced by Jack Christiansen. The 49ers have their worst season in their history: two wins and twelve losses.

1964 Vic Morabito dies of a heart attack, aged just 44. Josephine and Jane Morabito, widows of the two brothers, retain ownership and place the team's operations in the hands of Lou Spadia, general manager since 1952.

1968 Spadia takes over as president of the club and names Jack White as general manager. Dick Nolan succeeds Christiansen as head coach.

1970 Western Division champions, the first time in their 25-year history that the 49ers have won a title.

1971 Western Division champions.

1972 Western Division champions.
The 49ers lose to the Dallas Cowboys (coach Dick Nolan's former team) for the third time in a row in the NFC championship game.

1976 After the team has been in a slump for three years, Nolan is replaced by Monte Clark. The 49ers go on to have their first winning season since 1972.

1977 The 49ers are bought by Edward J. DeBartolo Jr, at 31 the youngest owner in the NFL.

1978 With a new coach (Pete McCulley) and many changes in the squad, the 49ers have the worst season in their history: 2–14. Midway through their disasters, McCulley is replaced by Fred O'Connor, who lasts only until the end of the season.

1979 Bill Walsh from Stanford University is appointed head coach.

Bill Walsh, one of the great coaches

1981 Western Division champions.

1982 NFC champions, defeating the Dallas Cowboys.
Super Bowl XVI champions, defeating the Cincinnati Bengals.

1983 Western Division champions.

1984 NFC champions.

1985 Super Bowl XIX champions, defeating the Miami Dolphins.

1986 Joe Montana has back surgery for a ruptured disc and doctors say he may never

★★★★★★★★ SUPERSTAR ★★★★★★★

Roger Craig
San Francisco 49ers

Setting Super Bowl records for points (18) and touchdowns (3), Roger Craig soared from relative anonymity straight into the spotlight of the nation's sports awareness. Commenting on his three touchdowns, 135-total offense performance in 1984's Super Bowl XIX, Craig calmly said 'Yes, it was definitely my best game as a pro . . . maybe not statistically, but for intensity and execution.' Some understatement! Super Bowl XIX was the final icing on a brilliant season for this fullback from Nebraska. He was the team leader with 71 receptions. Maybe it's a lucky talisman, being picked the 49th player to join the 49ers . . . at any rate the team's well pleased with its first choice in the 1983 selection. Bill Walsh certainly hasn't been sparing with his praise: 'Roger may well be the best all-purpose running back in the league. He has done everything we have asked of him, and equalled our expectations' — an accolade indeed. He certainly set a standard for the team; his reception yardage total established a single season standard for the 49ers running backs.

Wendell Tyler

Seattle Seahawks

5305 Lake Washington Boulevard, Kirkland, Washington 98033
(206) 827 9777

Stadium: Kingdome, 201 South King Street, Seattle, Washington 98104. 64,757 capacity; AstroTurf.

Conference: AFC (Western Division)

Colours: blue, green and silver

1974	The NFL awards a franchise to Seattle Professional Football Inc. — a group of business executives and community leaders — for $16 million. Lloyd W. Nordstrom and his family become majority shareholders.
1975	A contest is held to decide on the team's name. More than 20,000 entries are received, and 'Seahawks' is the winner, chosen by 151 entrants. On 28 July, the first day of season-ticket sales, 24,168 requests arrive; 27 days later an overwhelming 59,000 have been bought.
1976	Jack Patera, formerly of the Minnesota Vikings, is appointed the first head coach. The team play at the new $67 million Kingdome, the walls of which anchor the world's largest self-supporting concrete roof. The Seahawks finish their first season with a 2–12–0 record.
1977	The team improves its record to 5–9–0: the best of any previous second-year expansion team.

play again. However, he makes a miraculous recovery and returns 55 days later to throw for 270 yards and three touchdowns against the Cardinals. Against Washington, he launches the ball into the air 60 times and makes 441 yards, both new team records.

Wendell Tyler is released, but returns three weeks later because of injuries to other team members.

Western Division champions.

Hall of Fame members

Hugh McElhenny: back, 1952–60
Leo Nomellini: tackle/defensive tackle, 1950–63
Joe Perry: fullback, 1948–60, 1963
Y. A. Tittle: quarterback, 1951–60
John Henry Johnson: back

Seahawk quarterback Dave Krieg running with the ball

1978 After only three years the Seahawks have their first winning season: 9–7–0. Two of these victories are against the Oakland Raiders, the first time any team has beaten the Raiders twice during the regular season since 1965.

1980 Following another winning season, the Seahawks' defense collapses, allowing 408 points — the most in the AFC. The team finishes with a 4–12–0 record, including eight straight losses at the Kingdome.

1983 Patera having been replaced by Chuck Knox, who had successfully rebuilt both the Los Angeles Rams and the Buffalo Bills, the Seahawks go all the way to the play-offs — making Knox the first coach to take three different teams into the play-offs in NFL history.

1984 The team win a wild card spot in the divisional play-offs, where they defeat Super Bowl champions, the Los Angeles Raiders. The Seahawks are themselves beaten by the Miami Dolphins the following week.

After his two successful years with the team coach Knox is wooed by Henry Ford, a personal friend and owner of the Detroit Lions, who promises him part of that team if he will move to the Motor City. To keep him in Seattle, the Seahawk owners pay him an enormous sum.

1986 Steve Largent breaks Harold Carmichael's record of receptions in 127 straight games.

Tampa Bay Buccaneers

1 Buccaneer Place, Tampa, Florida 33607
(813) 870 2700

Stadium: Tampa Stadium, North Dale Mabry, Tampa, Florida 33607. 74,317 capacity; grass.

Conference: NFC (Central Division)

Colours: Florida orange, white and red

1974 Tampa Bay is awarded an NFL franchise, first to Philadelphia construction boss Tom McCloskey, who withdraws after two weeks, and then to Hugh F. Culverhouse, an attorney and property developer from Jacksonville, Florida, who pays $16 million.

1975 An advisory board headed by Culverhouse sifts through over 400 names for the team submitted by the public; the owner eventually settled on 'Buccaneers' (which was soon shortened to 'Bucks'), with a swashbuckling buccaneer for a logo.

1976 In their first season, the Bucks become the first team to have a 0–14 record (including five shut-outs) in NFL history, and also the first team to go winless since the Dallas Cowboys in 1960.

1977 After losing 12 games running in the new season, the Bucks finally have their first win on 11 December against the New Orleans Saints, ending a total winless streak of 26 consecutive games. More than 8,000 fans came out to welcome home the team.

1979 After such a dismal start, the Bucks gradually become much stronger and

Buccaneer running back James Wilder

more frequently victorious until, in a tiebreaker, they become Central Division champions.

1981 Central Division champions.

1983 Central Division champions (2 January).

1985 Worst record in NFL.

1986 Bucks finish with worst record in the NFL.

1987 Coach Leeman Bennett is fired and replaced by Ray Perkins, formerly on the coaching staff at the New York Giants.

Washington Redskins

Redskin Park, PO Box 17247, Dulles International Airport, Washington DC 20041
(703) 471 9100

Stadium: Robert F. Kennedy Stadium, East Capitol Street, Washington, DC 20003. 55,431 capacity; grass.

Colours: burgundy and gold

1932 The team is founded in Boston by a syndicate headed by George Preston Marshall of Washington DC, and named the Boston Braves after the baseball team whose field they use.
By the end of a mediocre 4–4–2 season and with a loss of $46,000, all the syndicate partners drop out except Marshall, who becomes sole owner.

1933 The team is moved to Fenway Park (home of the Red Sox baseball team), re-named the Boston Redskins and supplied with a full-blooded Indian coach — Will 'Lone Star' Dietz. For the team picture taken on the first day of practice the players all wear Indian headdresses, feathers and warpaint.
The team has so little money that, when the ball goes into the stands, owner Marshall approaches the stands and asks for it back.
Marshall suggests major rule changes (subsequently adopted by the NFL) which lead to a set schedule, two divisions with a championship play-off, moving the goal posts to the goal line and a slimmer ball to aid passing.

1936 Newly hired coach Ray Flaherty insists that Marshall stay off the field and in the stands.
Eastern Division champions.

1937 Team transferred to Washington, DC, to play at Griffith Stadium. Marshall organises elaborate half-time shows with marching bands.
Marshall signs Sammy Baugh, an All-America tailback, who in his 16 years with the team will set passing and punting records which still stand today.
Eastern Division champions, after a decisive win over the New York Giants (the second such game in two years). More than 10,000 Redskins fans travel to New York to see the game, then march up Broadway behind their band and overwhelm the Polo Grounds.
NFL champions, defeating the Chicago Bears.

1940 Before becoming Eastern Division champions, the Redskins defeat the Chicago Bears. The latter complain about some of the umpires' decisions, and Marshall retaliates by calling the Bears 'quitters' and 'crybabies'.
The Redskins lose the NFL championship game to the Bears, 73–0 — the most one-sided score in a championship game and the first to be broadcast coast-to-coast.

1941 During a home game in the nation's capital on 7 December, a number of high-ranking military men and government officials are called out of the stands, but it is not until the game is over that the crowd discovers that the Japanese have bombed Pearl Harbour and the US is at war.

1942 NFL champions, beating the Chicago Bears.

1943 Eastern Division champions, defeating

Art Monk
Washington Redskins

The date 1984, the number 106 — Art Monk made them both his own. George Orwell's *1984* might have kindled public imagination, but it's Redskins wide receiver Monk who can claim the year belonged to him. His sheer artistry on the field not only caught the imagination of the fans — who formed 'The Art Gallery' in his honour — it also presented them with the goods for real. 106 became a magical number for Monk — the number of catches he made during that classic year of 1984. In doing so he shattered the record of 101 catches established some 20 years earlier by Charlie Hennigan of the Houston Oilers and received the high praise: 'Art's year was the most valuable contribution I've ever seen by a wide receiver to his team,' from coach Joe Gibbs. 'He was always there to count on' was Joe Theismann's comment; indeed amidst a season of casualties, Monk never missed a play. And he certainly wasn't missed by the critics who, far and wide, applauded his skill with all-Pro selections by AP, UPI, *Pro Football Weekly*, Pro Football Writers' Association and the *Sporting News*. The Pro Bowl welcomed him for the first time and the Washington Touchdown Club and Quarterback Club voted him their player of the year. For not only did his magnificent 106 catches lead the NFL, his 1,372 yards were also good enough to place him fourth in the NFL and second in the NFC — totalling third best in club history!

Art's Pro career is undoubtedly one of distinction. A unanimous all-rookie selection in 1980, he soon proved his worth, breaking the club rookie receiving record which had been set in 1964 by Charlie Taylor. But that's not all Art Monk has pulled out of the bag for the Redskins. His 58 catches (for 797 yards) were tenth in the NFC and he enjoyed six games with five or more catches. His first NFL game (v Dallas) resulted in five catches for 55 yards and, keeping up this astonishing high level of play, his first NFL start was six catches for 85 yards (v St Louis). In 1981 Monk's 894 receiving yards were the most by any Redskin since 1967. In 1985 he set two new club records: 13 passes caught and 230 yards receiving. Add that to a winning streak of no fewer than 23 games where he caught at least one pass and it's all too easy to work out why the Redskins have reason to feel pleased with their first-round pick of 1980.

George Preston Marshall, who founded the team which became the Redskins. One of football's great showmen, he pioneered half-time entertainment, including introducing the first marching band, complete with Red Indian headdresses.

the New York Giants in a play-off.

1945 Eastern Division champions.

1949 With the Redskins producing mediocre football, there is much criticism in the sports press of Marshall's failure to hire any black players.

1950 The team become, with the Los Angeles Rams, the first to have all their games televised.

1952 After head coach Dick Todd resigns, saying he has received no respect, Marshall signs Earl 'Curly' Lambeau as Todd's successor.

1953 NFL champions, defeating the Philadelphia Eagles.
Lambeau retires after his 231st NFL victory.

1954 Dave Sparks, guard, dies of a heart attack after his team loses to the Cleveland Browns.

1956 Vic Janowicz, superb former All-America halfback, suffers irrevocable brain damage in a car accident during training camp.

1957 Roy Barni, defensive back, is shot dead in a bar-room brawl during training camp.

1961 The Redskins move to the new DC Stadium (later re-named Robert F. Kennedy Stadium), but the team still end the season with a 1–12 record.

1962 Marshall finally drafts his first black player, Ernie Davis, then transfers him for another black player, Bobby Mitchell. By the time the squad is complete, there are four black men on the team.

1964 Marshall signs quarterback Sonny Jurgensen.

George Rogers, running back

1965 In the biggest upset in their history, the Redskins fight back from a 21-point deficit to defeat the Dallas Cowboys 34–31, with Jurgensen passing for more than 400 yards and three touchdowns.
Cornerback Johnny Sample is suspended for insubordination.

1966 Otto Graham is appointed head coach and general manager.

1969 Legendary coach Vince Lombardi leaves Green Bay Packers to become part-owner, executive vice-president and head of the Redskins. He concentrates on developing the Redskins' running game (sadly lacking until then) and the team has its first winning season (7–5–2) since 1955.

The players, coaches, trainers and equipment staff of the Washington Redskins in 1985

Quarterback Jay Schroeder of the Redskins

1970 Lombardi dies of cancer at the beginning of the season.

1971 George Allen, former coach of the Los Angeles Rams, becomes head coach. He begins trading to obtain as many good veteran players as he can (including quarterback Billy Kilmer from the New Orleans Saints and linebacker Jack Pardee from the Rams), with the result that, by the end of the season, the team is known as the 'Over-the-Hill Gang'. This bunch of 'old men' give the Redskins their best record in 29 years (9–4–1).

1972 Eastern Division champions.
NFL champions, defeating the Dallas Cowboys.

1973 Runners-up at Super Bowl VII, losing to the Miami Dolphins.

1975 After celebrating his 40th birthday by leading the NFC in passing the previous year, Jurgensen retires after 11 years with the Redskins.

1976 Allen signs away his first draft choice to get quarterback Joe Theismann from the Miami Dolphins.

1978 George Allen leaves to return to the Rams and is replaced by former Redskins player and Chicago Bears coach Jack Pardee.
Guided by Theismann, the team has six victories in a row — the best start in the Redskins' history.

1979 Jack Pardee is named NFL coach of the year.

1981 After a losing season the previous year, Pardee is released and succeeded by Joe Gibbs.

1982 NFL champions.

1983 Super Bowl XVII champions, defeating the Miami Dolphins and earning their first world title in 41 years.

1984 NFC champions, defeating the San Francisco 49ers.

1985 Runners-up in Super Bowl XIX, losing to the Los Angeles Raiders by the largest margin in the history of the Super Bowl — 39–9.
John Riggins released, Joe Theismann breaks a leg.

1986 Enter the play-offs on a wild card.

Hall of Fame members

Cliff Battles: back, 1932–7
Sammy Baugh: halfback/quarterback/punter, 1937–52
Bill Dudley: back, 1950–1, 1953
Glen 'Turk' Edwards: 1932–40
Ray Flaherty: coach, 1937–42
Otto Graham: coach, 1966–8
Ken Houston: safety, 1973–80
Sam Huff: linebacker, 1964–7, 1969
David 'Deacon' Jones: defensive end, 1974
Earl 'Curly' Lambeau: coach, 1952–3
Vince Lombardi: coach, 1969–70
George Preston Marshall: owner, 1937–69
Wayne Millner: end, 1936–41, 1945

Don Shula, coach of the Miami Dolphins, has a distinctive Super Bowl record — one which he would care to forget. Along with Bud Grant, he holds the dubious distinction of suffering most defeats in a Super Bowl. He lost Super Bowl III when he was coaching the Baltimore Colts, and as coach of the Dolphins he has been defeated in Super Bowls VI, XVII and XIX.

UNIFORMS & EQUIPMENT

Curly Lambeau, the famous Green Bay Packers' coach and tailback wearing the minimal protective gear of the 1920s

Face guards on helmets come in various types, some favoured by players in different positions. The Houston Oilers' half cage guard (left) is a type preferred by many quarterbacks and running backs; the vertical bar on the Denver Broncos' helmet protects the nose

The NFL lays down very strict rules and guidelines as to the type of equipment and uniforms a team must have. To equip a team in all its uniform and equipment costs over $200,000 per season. All the equipment goes on the road with a team and you can understand why each team does 'a deal' with an airline for the whole season as their equipment alone weighs over 2,500 lb!

Shirts

All NFL teams must have one set of coloured playing shirts and one set of white. Up until a few years ago the league rule was that the home team wore coloured jerseys and the visiting team white, but now the rule is that the home team can choose. Some coaches prefer their teams to play in white because it makes the players appear bigger! Some players, especially offensive linemen, wear play-shirts that are too small so that defensive linemen won't have anything to grab on to, and running backs wear jerseys which will rip away if grabbed.

In 1973 the NFL introduced the now familiar numbering system for players.

1–19 — quarterbacks and kickers
20–49 — running and defensive backs
50–59 — centres and linebackers
60–79 — defensive linemen and interior offensive linemen
80–89 — wide receivers and tight ends
90–99 — defensive linemen

Helmets

The average life of a helmet is around three years, after which time it's so beaten up it's dumped or if a player wants to he can keep it as a memento of his action on the gridiron. The largest helmet is 8½, but a giant with a big head will have one tailored to suit — they cost nearly $200.

In 1978 the New York Jets changed to their now familiar 'Kelly' green garb. One reason was that they would be the only team in their division with green helmets and thus it would be easier for their quarterback to pick out his wide receivers! Helmets have gone through many changes since the flimsy leather 'Flying hats' worn in the early days. Now the helmets have air cells inside or cells filled with anti-freeze so that any impact is distributed evenly.

Bronco Nagurski, a 1930s great famous for his size and force wearing a primitive and inadequate helmet by today's standards

George Halas in his days as a player in the mid-1920s — laced trousers over protective gear were already being worn

Shoes

Since the advent of artificial turf, players' shoes have changed — there is, in fact a different kind of shoe for every kind of surface and every NFL player has a variety to choose from depending on the conditions. Receivers get through around three pairs a season — some cost as much as $150 a pair.

Padding

The NFL has rules that standardise the type of padding that players are permitted. They are shoulder pads, collar pads, thigh pads, knee pads, jockstrap, mouthpiece and helmet.

Each player has at least his ankles taped before a game or practice — other players tape almost every piece of their body — most teams use over 300 miles of adhesive tape during a season at a staggering cost of $30,000.

A player's mouth-guard is unique to each player. A wax impression of a player's mouth is taken so they can get a perfect fit. Not pleasant to have all that wax in your mouth, but better than having your teeth knocked out!

The ball

Finally, let's not forget the most important piece of equipment in the field, the one that everybody wants — the football.

Manufactured by the Wilson Sporting goods Company of Ohio, it sells for about $40 — it weighs 14–15 ounces and is inflated with 12½ –13½ pounds of air. Each pro ball bears the signature of NFL commissioner Pete Rozelle and the home team has to provide 24 footballs at every game. Most teams keep a stock of around 350!

Quarterback Bobby Douglas of the Chicago Bears scored four touchdowns on 4 November, 1973 — to do it he ran only 15 feet!

NFL protective equipment

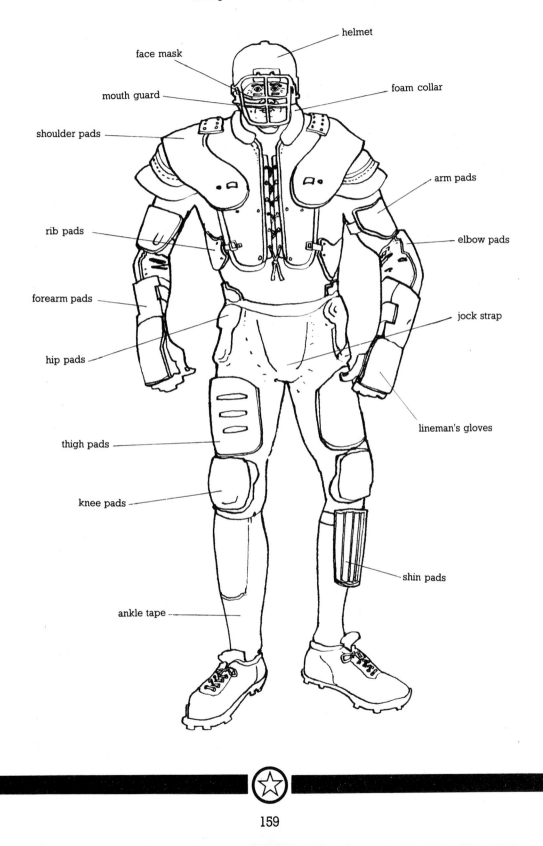

- helmet
- face mask
- mouth guard
- foam collar
- shoulder pads
- arm pads
- rib pads
- elbow pads
- forearm pads
- jock strap
- hip pads
- lineman's gloves
- thigh pads
- knee pads
- shin pads
- ankle tape

The early games of football were played in everyday clothes and without any body protection. It was impossible for people watching the game or quite often for the players themselves to work out what was going on.

The first recorded use of any form of uniform was in the game played in 1874 between Harvard and McGill. The Harvard team sported sweaters and handkerchiefs tied round their heads while McGill sported striped jerseys, white trousers and turbans.

Trousers were replaced by knee-length breeches, and at Yale no self-respecting player would be seen without his stocking cap with its distinctive pompom. In the 1887 season at Princeton, Leonidas P. Smock played football wearing a jersey with a large letter P on the front, canvas jacket, black canvas breeches and socks. This outfit was quickly taken up by the rest of the team and copied by other teams they played.

Not all the developments in uniforms were smiled upon. The 'flying wedge' formation created by Lorin F. Deland at Harvard caused mayhem on and off the field. Five players would dash forward and as the kicker nudged the ball they would pass him and he would follow with the ball behind this human battering ram. Players started to wear padding in an attempt to stop the wedge. The 'flying wedge' players then took to wearing jerseys with suitcase handles stitched on so that they had a better grip within the formation. There were so many deaths and injuries caused by this one play that it was outlawed after direct intervention by President Roosevelt in 1906.

Two years later the University of Pittsburgh introduced numbers sewn on to the players'

Shoulder padding weighs up to 5½ pounds, depending on the player's position: linemen wear the largest, wide receivers and players who need free arm movement for throwing wear rather less. Opposite is Broncos' number 20 Louis Wright.

jerseys as an aid in spotting who was who. Today this is still the case, and there is much debate over the practice of retiring the number of a star player when he retires from the game. The fear is that some teams will run out of numbers for certain positions and might have to use letters instead. One proposal is that on a favoured player's retirement his jersey should be sent to the Pro Football Hall of Fame so that the number can live on.

In 1921 the Acme Parking company, who owned what is known as the Green Bay Packers, spent $500 on jerseys with 'Acme Packers' sewn on the front. The first pro team to sport a team logo on its jerseys was the 1926 Duluth Eskimos who had an igloo in black and white sewn on.

Quarterback Yelberton Abraham Tittle is stuck with a rather unfortunate name but he's not alone — how about Buzz Nutter, Elmer Bighead, Vitamin T. Smith?

The Pittsburgh Steelers spent $1,400 for a football ejector — it can kick a ball 400 feet with the spin of a right- or left-footed kicker. What wouldn't a player give to be able to equal that?

Super Bowl V between the Baltimore Colts and the Dallas Cowboys stands as the 'Most Mistakes Bowl'. Baltimore lost possession four times on fumbles and three on interceptions. Dallas gave three interceptions and one fumble. So all in all there were 11 turnovers and no fewer than 14 penalties.

'War paint' used by the Washington Redskins as part of their image helped prevent glare, they found — and has now been adopted by players in other teams

In 1982 Super Bowl sponsors paid an estimated $1,000,000 per minute to bring their products to viewers' attention.

Buddy Young, who played for the Baltimore Colts, made many spectacular touchdowns. An Olympic-class sprinter, he relied on his amazing speed to keep his tiny 5 foot 5, $11\frac{1}{2}$ stone out of trouble and into victory.

As the game developed into a contact game so helmets and padding started to make an appearance. In many colleges at first this was not considered to be the done thing, but as the injuries and deaths continued so the protection developed. Helmets made of boiled leather started to appear but it was not until after the Second World War that they became a mandatory piece of kit. A company that had made helmets for American bomber crews in the Second World War found its market slump after the war. John T. Riddell's staff thought about it and produced a plastic helmet for footballers. It was a great success and has evolved into the classic teardrop shape used by all football teams today.

Houston Astrodome, opened in 1965, was the first roofed arena for clubs to do battle in. But it was the 72°F fixed temperature which made it an instant hit!

Tony Dorsett of the Dallas Cowboys holds the NFL record for the most consecutive seasons of gaining 1,000 or more yards (five from 1977–1981). And he's considered at 5 foot 11, and 13 stone a very small man to do the job.

FOOTBALL'S LOSS...

Gerald Ford became President of the USA in 1974. A full 40 years earlier, in 1934, he'd been a player in the University of Michigan football squad. And an outstanding player at that — named to the College All-Stars team which played the Chicago Bears in 1935.

THE COACH

Mike Ditka, head coach of the 1985 Super Bowl champions the Chicago Bears and named NFC coach of the year in 1986, took a mediocre team to greatness in four years. Ditka, born in 1939, became the Bears' tenth head coach in January 1982. He was one of the nation's leading college punters and in 1961 was the Bears' first-round draft choice and was named NFL rookie of the year. In 1964 he set an NFL record for tight ends by catching 75 passes. Ditka joined the Dallas Cowboys coaching staff in 1973, and he has played with the Philadelphia Eagles and the Dallas Cowboys as well as with the Chicago Bears, where he was tight end from 1961 to 1966.

I spoke to Ditka at his office at Halas Hall, just outside Chicago, in May 1986. A portrait of the legendary 'Papa Bear', George Halas, looked down from on high . . .

Nicky Horne: How much do you think you personally owe to George Halas?

Mike Ditka: Well, I think I owe everything because, you know, success in life comes through opportunities. I think there are a lot of capable people who never get a chance to show what they can do, and to have somebody who is in a position to give people an opportunity, to have the confidence in that person, to give them a break, that's a tremendous thing, and then to let them go ahead and do their job. So I would say that if I've got to thank somebody for my position today I would certainly have to thank Mr Halas for giving me the opportunity; then I'd have to thank myself for what I do with the opportunity.

NH: Indeed, but what about when you were offensive coach under Tom Landry, was he an important influence?

Ditka: Well, there's no question that he was — my whole coaching philosophy and what I understand and know about coaching and football from a coach's perspective came from Landry. I have tremendous respect for coach Landry and the Cowboy organisation; without him I wouldn't be here. But when you ask me how much Mr Halas played in it, he gave me that opportunity, the opportunity to coach. Coach Landry did the same thing; what he saw in me at that early age, I don't know, I really don't, because I was a football player, and I don't think I epitomised what a coach should be, but he gave me that chance to be an assistant coach and he trained me for nine years, and so he's played a tremendous role in my life.

NH: Then of course different coaches have different styles of leadership: Don Shula [Miami Dolphins] is known as a disciplinarian, Bill Parcells [New York Giants] is a bit of an extrovert, how would you describe your style of leadership?

Ditka: I don't think I have any one style, I believe very much in discipline, I believe very much in a team concept, I think everything has to be based on the value of the team, not the value of the individual as much. I understand that you must have great individuals within the concept of the team but the team must come first and the goals of the team must come first. Therefore I emphasise the complete aspects of team football —

Mike Ditka, dressed for the Chicago weather, watching a play in action from the sidelines

offense, defense and special teams, and I just don't like it when one aspect of it is emphasised more than another because I think you're going to get into problems after that. To me it's all a team concept. But I — as far as the discipline is concerned I think I'm a disciplinarian, I think I'm an extrovert in certain ways, I think I'm an introvert in certain ways. I don't mean that what I do is right or wrong, I just think that the main thing you've got to do in being a coach is be yourself . . .

NH: . . . and?

Ditka: . . . you have to know what you want to achieve, and I think you have to be able to relate to people. I think that people are the most important thing. How do you relate to them? How do you communicate with them? How do you get more out of them? I think those are the things you have to look for.

NH: Well, if those are the kind of qualities that you think you need for the job, you need to be sort of a mixture of a philosopher, a sergeant major, a psychiatrist, a strategist . . . what do you think is the most important quality? You said getting on with people, but getting on with people on so many different levels.

Ditka: The one thing that I've learned, and I probably took it from Halas and Landry, is not to be too rigid. I had to learn to be flexible, and I had to learn to change as moods changed, as people changed, as times changed. I don't know that there was any other one thing that's so important. I'd like to think that I have good qualities, of being fair to people, and I try to be consistent, I try not to be an up and down person with people, sometimes that's not easy to do, but those are qualities I look for in myself and try to improve in myself.

NH: You have been known to — to fly off the handle at your players.

Ditka: But flying off the handle has nothing to do with it; there's an interesting statement made that when you fly off the handle as a player you're called competitive, and when you fly off the handle as a coach you're called a hothead.

NH: . . . And you are both?

Ditka: Everybody has their way of showing what they feel; some people don't show what they feel and they usually drop dead. I happen to show what I feel, and whether it's appealing to people, or not, that's me, and that I don't try to hide. I wish at times that I didn't get as excited as I do, but yet that's *me*, and if I wasn't that way it wouldn't be me, and I would be a pretender, and I don't want to be that.

NH: You have no ulcers at the moment then?

Ditka: No ulcers . . .

NH: There's a poem by Walter D Wintle that Paul Bear Bryant used to put up in his locker room. Do you know *It's all in a state of mind*?

Ditka: Oh sure . . .

NH: Do you agree with that sentiment, 'if you think you'll lose you're lost for out in the world you'll find . . .'

Ditka: Look, it's here in front of me, 'It's all in a state of mind', I really believe that the key thing that we had to change when I came here was the attitude of the people. I think

Seven people are needed to control a pro football game. Until 1929 it was just three, then a tooter or field judge was added. In 1947 came the back judge and in 1965 the line judge. Finally in 1977 the seventh official was named — the side judge.

that everything you do in life is based on your attitude. I don't think that you'll ever be great at anything unless you have a good attitude about it. You have to seek greatness, you have to expect greatness, you have to anticipate greatness, you have to imagine greatness. Those are the things that I see, it's a state of mind, really. And the attitude is what makes it happen, it's a willingness in the mind to make the body do a lot of things, and I think once your will is convinced that something can happen, then your will can drive your body to do a lot of things it wouldn't normally do. That goes not only for football but for any sport — long-distance running, once that will kicks in and that mind is convinced that it can happen, that will move the body to extremes it hadn't really ever expected to go to. So I really believe in that very much.

NH: Let me move if I may from philosophy to strategy. When you're planning for a game, could you explain the procedure that you go through . . .

Ditka: Well, we go through a lot of study of movies. We study our own movies of course, previous to studying the opposition's movies to see if we're having tendencies or showing things that we don't particularly want to show a tendency for. Then we'll look at the opposition, we analyse what they're doing, by down-distance and situation, and it becomes a little technical, then we'll analyse what we're doing against what they're doing, where our strengths meet their weaknesses and vice versa, and all we try to do is, maybe make some changes, subtle changes, week to week, and decide what we do to complement our offense or defense against what the other team is doing. It's not a matter of rechanging every week a full-scale game-plan, because I think you're foolish if you do that. I think what you do is change the *look* of the way you do things, by formation or by a movement or by

some gimmick. But what you do is still based on how well you're going to execute the play. I'm a very strong believer in fundamentals and technique, and I think that the execution's the key. I don't care how you wrap the package, whether you wrap it in a fancy wrapping, or you wrap it in a plain wrapping; what it comes down to in the final analysis, is how well do you execute it? And that comes down again to what we talked about a few minutes ago — what's the attitude of the players? What do they believe they can execute? What do they want to do most out there? What do they enjoy doing most? If you're a team that has a certain type of offensive line you can't just throw the football every play and expect to be successful, our line thrives on running the football and that gives them their get up and go: that gets them ready to play; they love the run-block, and we have a great running back, so we run the football a lot more than most people, we're feeding them what they want. We still throw the football, but we know that our bread and butter is it. What I'm saying is that I try also to complement what our players do best.

NH: So how far ahead do you plan?

Ditka: Once we set a game-plan, and we set a game-plan early in the year out of our playbook — that game-plan could go the whole year with the changes we make weekly according to what we see. We will

What's it like to be a referee? One veteran NFI described his duties as 'trying to maintain order during a legalised gang brawl involving 80 toughs with a little whistle, a hanky and a ton of prayer' — ordeal by duty?

change some terminology week to week, or change a notable situation week to week, depending on the opposition. We feel that we can give our players three or four or five changes on offense or defense and not really boggle them down, but that when you come in and you start giving 20 or 25, then I think you start causing short-circuits and you don't get the production you really want.

NH: Do you use computerised technology to analyse the oppositions' play?

Ditka: Yes, we use it, and we use it very much. It's a main source of breaking down the opposition by down and distance and situation, without that it would be very hard to do by hand. We're very involved in that. We don't use the computer as much in the scouting end of it as the Cowboys do, but we do it in the football.

NH: That leads us nicely onto rookies. The training camp is going to be starting soon, and obviously with all the rookies coming in you have to be ruthless. Those rookies know that unless they make the grade they are out. That ruthlessness is part and parcel of the game. Is it difficult for you as a coach, when you have to call a player into your office and say 'sorry, son, you ain't going to make it.'

Ditka: That's the hardest thing there is; you never get used to it. I saw Tom Landry agonise about it in Dallas, and of course I agonise with it here. They tell me it gets easier as you coach longer, but I don't believe that. I think that you grow towards the players to a certain degree regardless of whether they really have an outside chance to make the team, or if they have a very good chance. What we do with our team is bring the rookies in and keep them a lot longer than most teams do, because we don't bring as many in. Therefore you see the person daily, you see them in meetings, you talk to them more, you become more familiar with them,

so it is a little bit harder when the time comes. The one thing we try to do is be honest with everybody and I think the players understand that. We've had very, very few cases where anybody really felt they were getting a bad deal; they realised that there were better players and that's why they were going. But that's always the hardest part of my job, I don't like that part of it . . .

NH: When you look at the scouting reports, coach, what do you look for first? — do you look for brawn, brains, emotion?

Ditka: Here's what I ask the scouts: 'First of all, tell me honestly, can the guy play football?' I mean that's what we're in, we're in the football business, right? And if the guy says he can play football, I ask him to tell me what kind of character he has, what kind of intelligence level he has, can he learn? Can he learn what we're going to teach him, is he a guy that can't learn? If he's a guy that can't learn then he doesn't fit our plans; if he's a guy that has a very poor character, as a person who is constantly in trouble with the law or in trouble with drugs or in trouble with something else then we'll stay away from him. So before I find out how big they are or how fast they run or any of that stuff I want to know the answer to those three questions. First of all is he a good player? Then does he have good character? And does he have a good intelligence level? Because if those things aren't there then I really don't care that much about him.

Just 15 coaches in pro history have won more than 100 games. Way out in the front is George Halas who coached the Chicago Bears to a cracking 326 victories.

NH: What was the best part of your coaching career? What's the best moment for you?

Ditka: Well, I hope the best hasn't come yet, I really do, but if you're going to talk about the best so far, I think the best was what I've seen happen in four years here. I've seen the fulfilment of my dream, of what I felt could happen, of moulding a group of men into a good football team, by getting the right kind of people, and that's what we did. We've got a very, very fine coaching staff, we've got a very fine group of people in management and I think we have excellent football players. And that wasn't true four years ago. But I do feel, regardless of what anybody wants to say or who they want to give credit to, that I am the architect of that whole scheme. The fact that we won 18 games last year, there are a lot of reasons for that, but I think, when you look at the kind of team we try to build, with the kind of attitude we try to have with our football team and the kind of ball we try to play, that's what I'm proud of — what we've accomplished over four years.

NH: In fact, I remember seeing you at the Conference championship press conference. When you got up at the podium I got the feeling that even *you* were surprised by the awesome power of the team that you created. . .

Ditka: . . . well . . .

NH: . . . was I right in that assumption?

Ditka: You were pretty close there. To shut out somebody in the play-off for a championship game, was such a thrill — it takes such a team effort to do that. What amazed me was that we had arrived on that upper echelon of football as a team . . . and to be able to shut the Rams and the Giants out (both very good teams), it did surprise me a little bit.

NH: It's going to be much more difficult next time round, isn't it?

Ditka: Well, if you do something good once then next time it's probably a little harder to do it again. The challenge is what counts and we've got a great challenge because we've lost coaches, we've lost some players and we're not favourites to do it again. Right now it's up to the players. I don't think our players are satisfied, that one championship has totally satisfied their hunger for winning. It's going to be fun, and I think the results can be as good if we go ahead and apply ourselves.

NH: Finally, if you weren't Mike Ditka, who would you like to be?

Ditka: If I wasn't Mike Ditka who would I like to be? Well, I would probably say if I wasn't Mike Ditka I would like to be President Reagan.

NH: Really? You have political aspirations?

Ditka: No, I'm not saying that I want to be the President. You asked me what would be satisfying to me in this point in my life, besides doing what I'm doing, and it would be doing what he's doing. He does it so well!

NH: Well, that's a great answer.

Football's Loss . . .

Who, in 1957 would have thought the 5'11" 12-stone end for the Pomona-Claremont Sagehens, would end up as a world famous singer? Pomona-Claremont were in the Southern California Conference and Kris Kristofferson was an outstanding player. His recording career was pretty successful as well.

THE HEADPHONES

One of the most frequent questions I get asked about American football is, 'why do most coaches wear headphones?' Well, they are not listening to soothing classical music — I can tell you that! The answer is simple: the head coach is in contact with his other specialist coaches, who are in a special box high in the stadium above the 50-yard line. These coaches each look at their own particular players — quarterbacks and wide receivers for one while another may concentrate just on the secondary. They analyse every play, and most teams now use computers which give detailed breakdowns of not only their team's play, but — more importantly — that of their opponents. These guys then communicate the information to the coach on the side-lines through his headphones.

These specialist coaches are separated from the frenzy of the game, and in the relatively quiet atmosphere of their box they can analyse the game more objectively. From their position they can see the whole area of play far better than the coach in the side-line can, and it is they who can turn a whole game around. For instance, if their computer tells them that their opponents have a tendency to run with the ball in certain situations, then they can counter that by making alterations to their game-plan.

Apart from computers, the coaches have a wide-angle camera always focused on the line of scrimmage. Every time the ball is snapped, they take a Polaroid photograph and study their opponents' formations. From these photographs they get a very good idea of the game-plan of the opposition. At half-time the players get to see the photographs, so they themselves get to see the 'whole picture'. Those guys in the box are the real 'chess players' — their strategy is all-important, so much so that there is an NFL rule stating that if one team's communications break down between the box and the sidelines, then the opposing team cannot use their system until the broken one is mended!

Bill Parcells, the New York Giants' head coach, listening to his coaches

Dan Reeves of the Denver Broncos not listening to his coaches

FOOTBALL'S LOSS...

Singer, actor and highly influential black activist Paul Robeson was one of the first standout players in NFL history and a consensus All-America at Rutgers State University in 1917 and 1918.

SUPERBOWL

If the unthinkable ever happened and the Russians wanted to launch a surprise attack on America, the day they would choose would be 'Super Sunday'. That is the day that America stops. Every town in America (except where the Super Bowl is being held) becomes a ghost town. The shops are shut, the streets are empty, cabs cannot be found, the crime rate plummets to almost nothing — all of America is at home watching the unique sporting and social spectacle.

Essentially it started on 15 January 1967 when the Green Bay Packers met the Kansas City Chiefs — the game's official title was the AFL-NFL World Championship. It was Lamar Hunt, the founding father of the AFL who christened the baby that has grown beyond even his wildest dreams. He got the idea from his daughter who was playing with a ball made of putty — she called it her 'Super Ball' — ball became bowl and Super Bowl it was. As a crowd puller Super Bowl I was not a success: only 61,946 people went to the 100,000 capacity Los Angeles Memorial Coliseum to watch the event. The ticket prices of $12, $8 and $6 were a bit steep and native Los Angeleans were not that exerted by the game.

It was in 1969 that the Super Bowl became a media event, and it was due to the talent and the personality of New York Jets' quarterback Joe Namath. He personally guaranteed that the Jets would win and become the first AFL team to become world champions.

Broadway Joe's 'guarantee' made all the press and television, and when the Jets did indeed win over the Baltimore Colts the AFL was no longer a 'Mickey Mouse' league, Namath was a hero and the modern Super Bowl hype had arrived.

Now, of course, the hype is unbelievable, even by American standards. In the week leading up to Super Bowl you cannot watch the television, listen to the radio, or read a paper without there being Super Bowl stories. The airwaves are thick with hype, and the city where the Super Bowl is being held becomes manic as the media and the fans descend.

I was in San Francisco for Super Bowl XIX in January 1985 and was lucky enough to be there a full week before the big day. 'Frisco is a vibrant wonderful city even without a Super Bowl, but to watch its vitality and energy grow as the hype took over was an incredible experience — everybody is gripped by Super Bowl fever. Of course for the city hosting the Bowl it means a massive income. January 1986's Super Bowl XX in New Orleans gave the city an income of over $100 million from 80,000 visitors spending an average $250 a day.

On the big day the fans at the game spent an average of $17.69 each on food and drink, as they munched their way through 28,500 hot dogs, 8,500 bags of peanuts, 16,500 bags of popcorn – and drank 36,000 soft drinks and 1,177 kegs of beer. The television audience of over 127 million people world-wide made it the largest viewing audience of an American television broadcast. That's more people than live in most countries . . .

Super Bowl is much, much more than a game of football . . .

The Super Bowl is uniquely American. It's more American than the 4th of July: the fireworks set off in its celebration were invented by the Chinese. It's more American than the inauguration of the Presidents — the pageantry of that is borrowed of course from their British cousins (Presidents don't have Roman numerals . . . Super Bowls do!) The Super Bowl is American through and through — the astronauts on Skylab III watched it from outer space; weddings have been cancelled when it was realised that the dates would clash with the Great Event; pregnant women have had their confinements induced the day before so they would not be in labour during the game! Super Bowl fever is indeed a potent force that has been created by the media and the NFL and to all intents and purposes is now bigger and more powerful than its creators — the lovable Frankenstein of sport! If for some reason Super Bowl didn't happen one year, the effect on America would be more devastating than another Watergate.

Super Bowl I

Green Bay Packers v Kansas City Chiefs (35–10)

Memorial Coliseum, Los Angeles, California; 15 January 1967
Green Bay scored first in this, the first official NFL championship game. It came after nine minutes of the first quarter when the Packers made 43 yards in five plays to the Chiefs' 37-yard line after an exchange of punts. And there was some entertaining play with Max McGee catching a pass in one hand balancing the ball on his hip, then outrunning the Chiefs to the end zone. In the second quarter the Chiefs tied the score 7–7. But favourites Green Bay, despite a setback when a 64-yard pass play that went for a touchdown was called back because a player was in motion before the snap of the ball, went to a convincing victory. Easy, then for the Packers' coach, the legendary Vince Lombardi, to say of the side his team had mauled, 'In my opinion, the Chiefs don't rate with the top names in NFL . . . they are a good football team with fine speed, but I'd have to say NFL football is better . . . that's what you wanted me to say, wasn't it?' It was certainly what the fans wanted to hear, after all the Packers had converted 10 of 14 third-down situations into firsts!

Vince Lombardi, widely held to be the best-ever pro football coach, after whom the Super Bowl winners' Vincent T Lombardi trophy is named

Super Bowl II

Green Bay Packers v Oakland Raiders (33–14)

Orange Bowl, Miami, Florida; 14 January 1968
'It wasn't our best,' said the Packers' coach Vince Lombardi. A hard man to please, Lombardi made this withering statement after his team's convincing win over Oakland. Maybe he was feeling jaded, because a few days after the match he announced that he was retiring as coach to concentrate on the job of general manager. What of this winning game which so disappointed the coach? The Packers were favourites from the start of the match, and their quarterback Bart Starr completed 13 of 24 passes for 202 yards and one touchdown, helping Green bay to convert 6 of 11 third-down situations into first downs. By half-time the Packers were leading 16–7, but it was in the second half that they really came into their own. They went 82 yards in 11 plays on their second possession; Danny Anderson scored a touchdown from the 2-yard line to push the score up to 23–7; Chandler's 31-yard field goal made it up to 26–7 at the end of the third quarter; during the fourth quarter Herb Adderley ran for 60 yards to make Green Bay's final touchdown. Oakland made a last-ditch fight back scoring the final touchdown with nine minutes 13 seconds remaining in the game. It didn't seem such a terrible effort from the Packers, but Lombardi was adamant: 'All year it seemed like as soon as we got a couple of touchdowns ahead we let up. Maybe that's the sign of a veteran team, such as ours. I don't know.' But perhaps after all his statement was prophetic — the Green Bay Packers have never since made the coveted Super Bowl.

Super Bowl III

New York Jets v Baltimore Colts (16–7)

Orange Bowl, Miami, Florida; 12 January 1969
Although considered one of the greatest teams in the 49-year history of the NFL, the Baltimore Colts were well and truly beaten by the New York Jets. The win made the Jets the first AFL team to beat an NFL team in the Super Bowl. Jets quarterback Joe Namath had stuck his neck out at an award dinner three days before the match with a speech which made the national headlines: 'This should be a most valuable player award for the entire team. You can be the greatest athlete in the entire world, but if you don't win football games, it doesn't mean anything . . . And we're going to win on Sunday, I'll guarantee you.' To understand just how bold this statement was you must realise that the predictions were running very much against him. Some thought the Colts would win 55–0, others a marginally more conservative 48–0. At any rate, as far as the experts were concerned, the odds were definitely against the Jets. However, the Jets snatched an early lead and with Namath completing four of five passes for 43 yards including one pass of 12 yards to Snell; Snell going 35 yards in six carries during the drive; and field goals of 32, 30 and 9 yards from Tumir, they had established a 16–0 lead in the fourth quarter. With a final score 16–7, the Colts had narrowly avoided a complete duck. Baltimore coach Don Shula was forced to admit 'We didn't make the big plays we have all season . . . we just didn't do it . . . they deserve the victory.'

Joe Namath of the New York Jets showing the form which earned him the most valuable player in Super Bowl III title

Super Bowl IV

Kansas City Chiefs v Minnesota Vikings (23–7)

Tulane Stadium, New Orleans, Louisiana; 11 January 1970

Underdogs Kansas City emerged victorious from the Super Bowl IV scrap with the Minnesota Vikings, although the AFL Chiefs were thought to have little chance against the heavily favoured NFL Vikings. To add spice and tension, the match was surrounded with intrigue. Chiefs' quarterback Len Dawson was linked to a gambling investigation — eventually his name was cleared just five days before the match, but the attention made him the talk of the game. He came up with the goods (despite having missed the main season games due to a knee injury), completing 12 of 17 passes for 142 yards and one touchdown. Right from the start the Chiefs led the way. The very first time they had the ball they marched 42 yards to Jan Stenerud's 48-yard field goal and moved 55 yards to Stenerud's 32-yard field goal on their second possession. The streak held, and on third possession they went 27 yards to Stenerud's 25-yard field goal. The scene was set, Kansas City led 9–0 and they played it all the way to a convincing victory. After the game Dawson said 'The best thing about this game is that we don't have to answer for it for the next three years' (referring to their defeat by the Green Bay Packers in the first Super Bowl). He then went away to answer a telephone call — President Richard Nixon was on the line!

☆ *Football's Loss . . .*

Bill Cosby played collegiate football during the 1960s seeing plenty of action in the Owl's backfield. In 1961 he averaged 3.5 yards per carry on 36 rushing attempts for the Owls who posted a 2–5–2 record. And none of these years are lost for Cosby who draws on his reminiscences and football stories for his popular comic routines.

Super Bowl V

Baltimore Colts v Dallas Cowboys (16–3)

Orange Bowl, Miami, Florida; 17 January 1971

Tom Nowatzke scored on the Colts' second play during the fourth quarter. That, together with Jim O'Brien's point after touchdown, was enough to bring Baltimore level with Dallas 13–13. With only 6 minutes 35 seconds left in the game it seemed Super Bowl V was to be a tie, but with five seconds left O'Brien made the kick of a lifetime. 'Just kick the ball straight', had been his team mate Earl Morrall's advice; everyone held their breath as the ball spun through the air, end over end, curving towards the right goal post, then miraculously (and there was no wind) it veered back to the middle and through the uprights. It was all over and the Baltimore Colts had won. When it was suggested to player Bob Vogel that the Colts were very lucky indeed, he was ready with a sharp answer: 'So what? . . . We deserve it!'

★

In 1976 a tornado deflated the Silverdome by 105 feet — but the game went on!

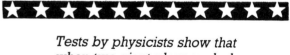

Tests by physicists show that when two giant players clash at headlong speed, the kinetic energy they release could move 33 tons one inch.

Jim O'Brien kicking the sensational 32-yard field goal which gave the Colts victory over the Cowboys in the last five seconds of Super Bowl V

Super Bowl VI

Dallas Cowboys v Miami Dolphins (24–3)

Tulane Stadium, New Orleans, Louisiana; 16 January 1972

Beaten at the post during the last few seconds of Super Bowl V, the Dallas Cowboys were back for a second consecutive attempt in Super Bowl VI, this time against the Miami Dolphins. It could have been little consolation to coach Don Shula (his Baltimore team had been beaten in Super Bowl III by the New York Jets) that not only did his tactics not pay off, but neither did those suggested by President Richard Nixon. Nixon had phoned Shula before the match with the advice that 'The Cowboys are a good defensive team but I think you can hit Paul Warfield on that down-and-in pattern.' Warfield was the Dolphin's wide receiver but his pattern had been spotted by the Cowboys who double-teamed him. 'We made sure they didn't complete that pass on us' said Cowboy coach Tom Landry. Which only goes to show, it really doesn't do to become predictable in pro football!

Super Bowl VII

Miami Dolphins v Washington Redskins (14–7)

Memorial Coliseum, Los Angeles, California; 14 January 1973

Having been well and truly drowned in Super Bowl VI, the Dolphins must have been given a stern talking to by coach Don Shula who, fast developing a reputation for losing Super Bowls, desperately needed his team to make the grade this time. And it was certainly a season where so far they'd made the grade all the way. The Super Bowl victory over the Washington Redskins completed an outstanding season in which they won all their 17 games — a professional football record. Shula could breath a sigh of relief. 'The pressure's off' he said. But although line-backer and co-captain of the Redskins Jack Pardee can be quoted as saying 'We were never really in the game . . .', it has to be said that Miami lost opportunities and made mistakes, most notably a blunder at the end of the game by Garo Yepremian. Garo said afterwards 'This is the first time the goat of game is in the winner's locker room . . . I should have fallen on the ball, but my mind went blank.' Well maybe, but there was nevertheless plenty to celebrate in that locker room that afternoon!

Super Bowl VIII

Miami Dolphins v Minnesota Vikings (24–7)

Rice Stadium, Houston, Texas; 13 January 1974

Miami and Minnesota both set records in Super Bowl VIII — Miami by appearing for the third time, Minnesota by losing for the second. The Dolphins took control on the first series of offensive plays. In polishing off this, their second consecutive Super Bowl contest, the Dolphins were asked how they thought they compared with the pace-setting Packers. Larry Csonka was dismissive, 'I don't know about legends or statistics,' he said, 'Football is a "now" game; that's all that matters.' Well maybe, but like the great Packers before them, the Dolphins have fallen from grace and have never since made the Super Bowl.

Pittsburgh Steeler Lynn Swann making the spectacular winning catch in Super Bowl X from Terry Bradshaw's touchdown pass

Super Bowl IX

Pittsburgh Steelers v Minnesota Vikings (16–6)

Tulane Stadium, New Orleans, Louisiana; 12 January 1975

Pittsburgh fullback Franco Harris set Super Bowl records by rushing 34 times for 158 yards. What's more, it was the Steelers' first championship in their 42-year history. The Vikings had reason to feel the real cutting edge of the Steelers; it was, after all, Minnesota's third Super Bowl defeat. Things didn't look too black at half-time: the Steelers 2–0 could easily have been overcome. But the Vikings were simply outclassed, with the Steelers seemingly able to confuse them at will; Pittsburgh outgamed Minnesota 333–119 in total offense with both Harris and Bleier finding gaping holes in the Viking defense. Much of their effort was directed against Minnesota's centre, Mick Tingelhoff. On defense the Steelers put a man directly over Tingelhoff and Ernie Holmes at times attacked him directly. Fran Tarkenton was also an objective — indeed so good was the Steelers' cover that he completed just 11 out of 26 passes for 102 yards with three interceptions; four attempts were deflected and many others thrown under pressure. No one could say the Steelers stole Super Bowl IX — they won it fair and square.

★

Super Bowl X

Pittsburgh Steelers v Dallas Cowboys (21–17)

Orange Bowl, Miami, Florida; 18 January 1976

Pittsburgh and Dallas had each won a Super Bowl; each was ready to fight it out. The match was loaded with tension, but the real drama came in the last few minutes of the game. Pittsburgh quarterback Terry Bradshaw threw a pass covering 59 yards to wide receiver Lynn Swann; Swann carried the ball the remaining 5 yards for a 64-yard touchdown — the points gained proved crucial for the Steelers' victory. But Bradshaw didn't see that important catch — he'd been knocked unconscious by Cowboy Cliff Harris — and it was not on the pitch but in the dressing room that he learnt that his pass to Swann had gone for a very important touchdown.

★

Super Bowl XI

Oakland Raiders v Minnesota Vikings (32–14)

Rose Bowl, Pasedena, California; 9 January 1977

For the fourth time Minnesota was in Super Bowl contention — but for the fourth time failed to win on the day. Obviously a decisive victory for Oakland, but their quarterback Ken Stabler took it all in his stride, 'When you've got the horses, you ride them,' he said, referring to Art Shell and Gene Upshaw, 'we're not a fancy team. We just line up and try to knock you out of there. Nobody's better at it than those two guys.' Fair enough comment, but what's wrong with taking pleasure in victory. After all, Oakland hasn't made an appearance in the Super Bowl for nine years!

Joe Schmidt (Detroit Lions) had his own special form of violence. He tore the trousers off Rams quarterback Roman Gabriel with his hands and teeth.

Butch Johnson's diving touchdown catch in Super Bowl XII which went towards the Cowboys' final score of 27

Super Bowl XII

Dallas Cowboys v Denver Broncos (27–10)

Louisiana Superdome, New Orleans, Louisiana; 15 January 1978

'They played the kind of game we usually play,' said Broncos' quarterback Craig Morton. 'They beat us at our own game — taking turnovers.' Well, that's one way to explain a crushing defeat! The first half was totally controlled by the Dallas Cowboys' defense who intercepted four passes and succeeded in recovering three fumbles. The Cowboys managed to convert two of the interceptions into 10 points which helped build a strong 13–0 half-time lead. Their confidence running high, the Cowboys marched on to build up a stunning 20–3 lead. Four plays later that lead had been cut to 20–10 as Bronco Norris Weese sent Rob Lytle off the left side of the line for a one-yard touchdown. But the Cowboys' concentration held and the Broncos failed to claw back points. The final score was devastating. The Cowboys dominated the statistics too, running up 325 yards to 156 for the Broncos. Roger Staubach completed 17 of 25 for 183 yards and one touchdown. The Dallas defense held Morton to 19 net yards' passing and four intercepted passes, while Weese ended with just 16 net yards passing. All in all, there wasn't a lot else Morton could have said other than: 'So many times this season other teams gave us all the turnovers. Today it was just our turn!'

John Stallworth's famous catch from a 73-yard pass in Super Bowl XIV put the Steelers in the lead, which they held to the end

Super Bowl XIII

Pittsburgh Steelers v Dallas Cowboys (35–31)

Orange Bowl, Miami, Florida; 21 January 1979
Super Bowl XIII saw a battle of veterans. Both knew what it was like to win; only the Cowboys knew what it felt like to lose. But, though a hard-fought contest recording the highest ever Super Bowl points, the team from Dallas was to be once again disappointed as the Steelers collected their third Super Bowl. Not that Dallas had anything to be ashamed of; its offense netted 330 yards — only 27 fewer than the Steelers. The Cowboys made just one real error — tight end Jackie Smith dropped a pass. From then on the Steelers seemed in control. Said Dallas coach Tom Landry: 'We were coming back until the Smith play. That play really swung the momentum. You can tell how much it hurt us by looking at the difference in the score. Then at the end of the game there was just too much to make up in too little time — our offense couldn't quite do it.'

The longest touchdown reception ever in a Super Bowl — Kenny King receives from fellow Oakland Raider Jim Plunkett in Super Bowl XV

Super Bowl XIV

Pittsburgh Steelers v Los Angeles Rams (31–19)

Rose Bowl, Pasadena, California; 20 January 1980

It looked as if the Steelers were going to fail to bring off their fourth Super Bowl win in as many appearances. Then, at the beginning of a tension-loaded fourth quarter, they came up from behind with John Stallworth receiving a 73-yard touchdown pass from quarterback Terry Bradshaw, followed up with a second hit to Stallworth with a 45-yard pass to set up an insur-ance touchdown. The result was a decisive victory for Pittsburgh. It was a hard pill for the Rams to swallow; at half-time they'd entered the locker room with a 13–10 lead. Not a huge advantage maybe, but enough to give them confidence that they were in with a chance of cracking the seemingly invincible Steelers. The statistics at half-time were close; the Rams led in total yards 130 to 127, each team had nine first downs, and the only turnover was Elmendorf's interception. The Steelers were razor sharp in the second half, quickly getting back on top. But the Rams fought back, and struck up a 19–17 lead. Then along came Bradshaw and the rest is history.

John Riggins, Redskins' fullback, in a fourth touchdown run in Super Bowl XVII, part of his record-making fourth consecutive 100-yard rushing game

Super Bowl XV

Oakland Raiders v Philadelphia Eagles (27–10)

Louisiana Superdome, New Orleans, Louisiana; 25 January 1981

Oakland, making their third Super Bowl appearance, took early control of the match. Line backer Rod Martin, on the third play of the game, intercepted Ron Jaworski's pass on the Philadelphia 47-yard line, returning it to the 30. Seven plays later Raider Jim Plunkett threw a touchdown pass. It was certainly a day to remember for Plunkett. His coach Tom Flores said: 'All Jim needed was someone to believe in

him . . . Out there today he could accomplish almost anything he wanted. He was the key for us the whole way.' And there was more than just praise for Plunkett — honours came his way too — he was voted the most valuable player in the game after completing 13 of 21 for 261 yards and three touchdowns. The only touchdown of the match for the Eagles came at the start of the fourth quarter from Jaworski, who capped a 12-play 88-yard drive with an 8-yard pass to tight end Keith Krepfle. Eager the Eagles might have been, successful they were not. The final result made the record books — it was the first time a Super Bowl had been won by a wild card team.

The Super Bowl record-breaking 74-yard touchdown run by Los Angeles Raider Marcus Allen in Super Bowl XVIII

Super Bowl XVI

San Francisco 49ers v Cincinnati Bengals (26–21)

Pontiac Silver Dome, Michigan; 24 January 1982

Neither team had been in a Super Bowl before; both desperately wanted to win and the game was hard fought. Though the 49ers were victorious, it was the Bengals who dominated the statistics, holding a 356–275 yardage edge. Quarterback Ken Anderson completed a rec-

ord 25 of 34 passes for 300 yards and two touchdowns, both to Dan Ross who set a Super Bowl Mark with 11 receptions. However, it was 49er Joe Montana who was named most valuable player. He threw for 157 yards and one touchdown, completing 14 of 22 passes. But it was San Francisco's defense which came up with the big plays throughout the game, including a four-play goal-line stand late in the third quarter, successfully staving off the Bengals offensive.

San Francisco 49er Joe Montana, Super Bowl XIX's most valuable player, in a touchdown scramble

Super Bowl XVII

Washington Redskins v Miami Dolphins (27–17)

Rose Bowl, Pasadena, California; 30 January 1983

'Ron may be president but tonight I'm king' said Super Bowl XVII's most valuable player John Riggins as Washington swept to victory over the Miami Dolphins. It was Riggins' power that overcame the Dolphins, as he rushed for a Super Bowl record 166 yards or 38 carries and he scored a game-winning touchdown that will be remembered for years for its power, brilliance and style. It was on a Redskin fourth down — there was 10 minutes left on the clock. Redskins' quarterback Joe Theismann handed the ball off to 'Old Diesel' Riggins, who ran all of 43 yards to score. It was Riggins' finest moment.

The Redskins' defense was leak-proof in the second half, allowing the Dolphins only 34 rushing yards and zero passing yards. In total yardage Washington were supreme 400–176.

Don Shula, the Dolphins' coach played a fairly orthodox game but Joe Gibb's plan was by far the better — let Theismann throw and let Riggins run. It worked a treat. The Redskins got the Lombardi Trophy, the Super Bowl rings and a live phone call — televised of course, from the President, Ronald Reagan.

186

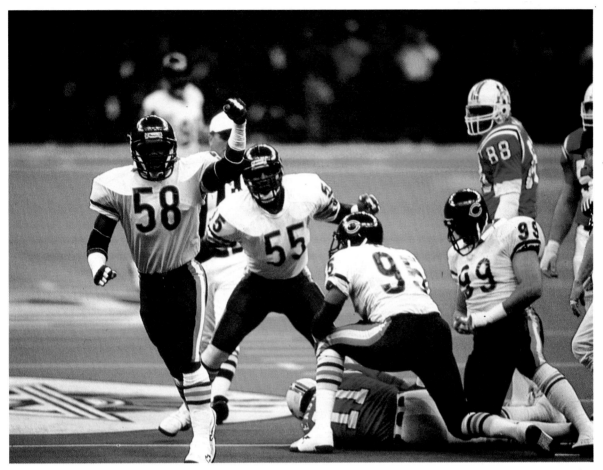

The Chicago Bears' defense showing domination in Super Bowl XX

Super Bowl XVIII

Los Angeles Raiders v Washington Redskins (38–9)

Tampa Stadium, Tampa Bay, Florida;
22 January 1984

Very few teams have ever made it to the Super Bowl in consecutive years — Green Bay, Dallas, Miami and Pittsburgh and with the exception of Dallas they have all seen two victories. So would Washington join the elite?

I was in Tampa Bay the week before the game — it was my first time at a Super Bowl, as the previous year I had been in a London studio. It was an incredible experience even in Tampa, which is not the greatest of places. In the run-up to the game it was Washington who did all the talking — Joe Theismann in particular — and it did without doubt affect their game. The LA Raiders on the other hand kept themselves to themselves and when the big day came the Raiders dominated. Their 38–9 victory was then the largest winning margin in Super Bowl history. Victory was built around the remarkable talents of Marcus Allen, who rushed for a Super Bowl record 191 yards and two touchdowns. He scored twice in the second quarter and his second run of 74 yards, a remarkable effort, was the longest run in Super Bowl history.

The Raiders' defense was awesome — Theismann had a rotten day and by half-time they were 21–3 in the lead. The Redskins never recovered and instead of entering the record books as one of the elite to win consecutive Super Bowls they went down as the team who had lost by the most points!

Super Bowl XIX

San Francisco 49ers v Miami Dolphins (38–16)

Stanford Stadium, California; 20 January 1985
I was lucky enough to be in San Francisco for this one and boy, what a time we had.

We arrived a full week before the game and as soon as we touched down we started working. The city, one of my favourites in the world, was vibrant, the 49ers had had a near perfect season and they were playing on home ground — the city got wilder and wilder as the week progressed.

This was tabled as the finest match-up of recent memory — the two teams were without any shadow of a doubt the best in the business. This was the best against the best: two gifted quarterbacks, Joe Montana versus the precocious talents of Dan Marino; coach Bill Wash against the genius of Don Shula; two teams who were at their very peak. The 49ers, although marginal favourites had *never* beaten the Dolphins. This was going to be one hell of a game. In the event it did not quite live up to its promise. Why?

Well, in the week proceeding the Super Bowl most of the talking was done by Dan Marino who had the press round him like flies, whereas the 49ers kept as quiet as they could. I think the build up and the day got to Marino. I'll always remember at the very beginning of the game a shot of Marino winking at the camera as if to say — 'We've got this one in the bag.' Without being unduly unfair I think he got too cocky!

The 49ers, on the other hand, were a perfectly balanced team with no significant weakness. Joe Montana loves to scramble and run with the ball, Marino doesn't. On that day Montana was the perfect field general galvanising his team in a display of power and beauty that was astonishing to watch.

Late in the first half the Dolphins had a chance to get back into the game but Marino could not get into gear. The score at half-time was 28–10.

In the third quarter the 49ers were racing ahead 38–16 and that was the final score. Joe Montana became only the third player in Super Bowl history to be voted most valuable player in two different Super Bowls and the 49ers carried off the Vince Lombardi trophy with style and aplomb. The Dolphins, tails between their legs, boarded their chartered 747 and had a very, very long flight back to Miami.

★

Super Bowl XX

Chicago Bears v New England Patriots (46–10)

Louisiana Superdome, New Orleans, Louisiana; 26 January 1986
Super Bowls are hyperbole and hype, and this one was no exception. The Chicago Bears were there because they were simply the best team by far in the NFL.

Their opponents on the other hand were there not because they were the best team in the AFL — they *were* statistically, but they were there through luck and a following wind and the fumbles of others; they were a good team, but they were not in the same universe as the Bears. Super Bowl should be 'the best against the best' — and this Super Bowl was the 'best' against 'the good'.

No one seriously gave the Patriots a chance and when the game started the result, barring injuries to the Bears' key players, was a foregone conclusion.

Then things changed . . . a bit. The Patriots scored first — a field goal. We all rushed to our record books. 'The team that scores first in the Super Bowl normally goes on to win.' We sat up and took notice. But there are lies, damned lies and statistics. These three points only served to concentrate the Bears' collective mind. The Bears wanted a shut-out — now they could go for the longest margin of victory ever seen in a Super Bowl.

It's all in a state of mind, and from that moment the Bears were unstoppable. Touchdown followed touchdown — their defense was impregnable — astonishing. It was as if the Bears were on a touchdown shopping spree — it turned out to be the Bears Picnic. Once they were invincible they took life easy — Jim McMahon was rested and coach Ditka gave William Perry what he (and his agents) wanted most — a Super Bowl touchdown. The moment Perry crossed the line his fees doubled.

Super Bowl XX was a bitter disappointment — its redeeming feature was the astonishing display of dominance by the Bears.

Super Bowl XX was a lesson in annihilation.

Super Bowl XXI

New York Giants v Denver Broncos (39–20)

Rose Bowl, Pasadena, California; 25 January 1987

While being nowhere near as one-sided as Super Bowl XX, 1987's showpiece had its firm favourite and definite underdog. The Giants had gone from strength to strength all season and had grabbed the New York headlines from the early season revelations, the Jets.

The Big Apple was still buzzing from the Mets' win in the baseball World Series and New Yorkers were not alone in believing there was more sporting glory to come to that great city.

Players like Joe Morris, Phil Simms and the leader of the New York Sack Exchange, Lawrence Taylor, had grown in stature throughout the season as the Giants claimed their first divisional championship for 23 years.

The Broncos had arrived in Pasadena after a

season of wavering fortunes. An impressive start led to mid-term hiccups, before a strong closing burst. Their precocious and enormously talented quarterback John Elway was a potential match winner, but would be severely tested by the mighty Giant defense.

Rich Karlis, Denver's bare-footed kicker, notched the longest field goal in Super Bowl history, when he opened the scoring from 48 yards. Simms found Zeke Mowatt to snatch the lead for New York, before Elway himself rushed over to return the advantage to Denver.

In the second quarter Elway took his team to first and goal with the prospect of taking a 17–7 lead. The New York defense showed its mettle and the net result was a five-yard loss. To make matters worse, Karlis fluffed the 23-yard kick to claim a second Super Bowl record, that of the shortest field goal missed.

An injury to Denver's defensive inspiration, Tom Jackson, a safety on Elway and another missed field goal compounded the Bronco's misery. With a slender one point lead at the half, their spirit was all but broken.

If they were looking for sympathy, the Giants were in no mood to give it. At the end of the third quarter New York had turned in one of the best 15 minutes in their history to take the score to 26–10.

Back up wide receiver Phil McConkey tidied up for a touchdown, after a juggling act by Mark Bavaro and Ottis Anderson sealed matters with a late score. By the time Elway crowned an exceptional personal performance with a 47-yard touchdown pass to Vance Johnson, the game was already over.

The young quarterback's individual brilliance was no match for an awesome team show by the Giants and that night the Empire State Building looked magnificent, decked out in the distinctive and victorious blue, white and red. The Vince Lombardi Trophy was now in Giant hands!

THE ZEBRAS

An American football game is contested by two teams — right? But there is another team out there on the field — the Zebras — those guys with the striped shirts and the yellow hankies. The officials.

There are seven officials at each NFL game and these are their jobs.

Referee

The boss — he signals all fouls and is the final court of appeal on the interpretation of the 1,800

It's a touchdown: — signalled by a zebra

rules in the 210-page rule book. He can impose penalties on players and coaches found guilty of unsportsmanlike conduct and he can throw a player off the field — not literally of course.

Umpire
He looks for false starts at the line of scrimmage and checks on line blocking to see it's legal.

Head linesman
Keeps a check on the line of scrimmage, keeps track of downs and supervises the 'chain gang'.

Line judge
He observes wide receivers on his side and keeps time of the game.

Side judge
Shares a lot of responsibility with the back judge looking for illegal blocks, loose balls, etc.

The officials get paid by the NFL — around $1,000 a game depending on their experience and in a season they travel over 125,000 miles. A small percentage are ex-players but the rest come from all walks of life, bankers, policemen (naturally), teachers, doctors.

Back judge
He's on the same side as the line judge — looks at the tight end and looks for holding, illegal use of hands, pass interference and out of bounds.

Common official signals

incomplete pass, penalty refused, missed kick

illegal motion

first down

delay of game

pass interference

personal foul

time out

offside or encroaching

illegal use of hands

holding

touchdown, field goal

illegal contact

Field judge

Stays 25 yards downfield. Watches for holding and blocking violations, times the 30-second clock and is the guy who signals if a field goal is good or not.

Where Officials Stand

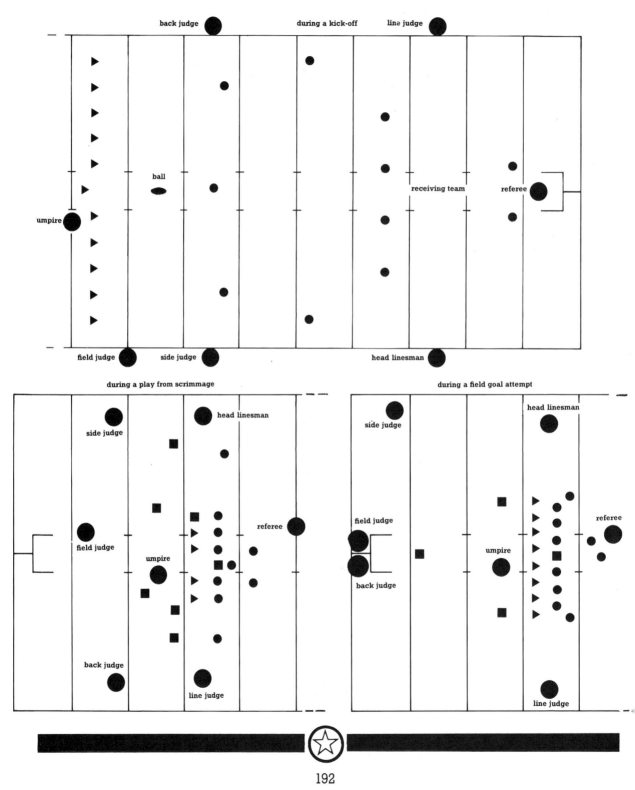

One good thing about American pro football is you can retire at an early age. And that's exactly what Jim Brown did in 1965, aged 29, after turning in a 1,554-yard rushing season for the Cleveland Browns. He began a new career, this time in the glamorous world of Hollywood where his rugged physique was snapped up by producers for such films as *Rio Conchos*, *The Dirty Dozen*, *Ice Station Zebra* and *100 Rifles*.

NATIONAL FOOTBALL LEAGUE

From its office on Park Avenue in New York the National Football League administers the most efficient, professional and lucrative sporting corporation in the world. It's also one of the most powerful business organisations in the USA.

'The League' controls not only the teams, but the whole game, from approving t-shirts to negotiating billion dollar tv contracts, from choosing the officials, to donating money to charity. It is indeed a formidable organisation wielding immense power over players and fans alike. Let's look inside the NFL.

NFL Management Council

Headed by an executive committee consisting of the owners/presidents of the Tampa Bay Buccaneers, Cincinnati Bengals, Pittsburgh Steelers, New England Patriots, Miami Dolphins, and the Dallas Cowboys — they work closely with the representatives of the players' own union, the Players Association, ensuring that the now exemplary relationship between the NFL and the players is maintained and strengthened.

The Players Association has done very well for its players, increasing a rookie's average salary from $34,000 in 1977 to around $70,000 in 1982. In 1984 the average salary for all players in the NFL was $163,000. But a player's average salary doesn't stop there by a long way: adding pre- and post-season play, plus incentive bonuses, the average player received another $20,000 in

1984. The average salary does not include around $50,000 in extra benefits, such as medical and disability insurance. This is how the extra money broke down in 1985: from the first day of training camp in late summer rookies got $425 a week and veterans $475 a week, plus $200 for every pre-season game until the start of the regular season.

But it's in post-season play that the money really starts flying in. In 1985 the NFL's post-season fund was $12.8 million — that money was divided among the 581 players who were lucky enough to play for more than the 16-week main season between September and Christmas. Now the incentives increase dramatically as post-season play advances. The Super Bowl of course brings its own special rewards. In Super Bowl XX when the Chicago Bears beat the New England Patriots each Bear player received $64,000.

One benefit unique in professional sports is that of severance pay. Any player who has played two or more seasons in the NFL is eligible for severance payment if he is cut or retires. For instance, a player whose been in the NFL for four years receives $70,000, rising to a whopping $150,000 for 12-year veterans: the NFL takes good care of its players!

NFL Officials

There are currently 107 NFL game officials, all of whom are paid for and administered by the NFL. The officials are quite well paid, getting

Pete Rozelle, NFL commissioner since 1960 and a 1985 entrant to the Hall of Fame

between $450 and $1,200 for every regular season game, and $5,000 for officiating the Super Bowl. Remaining an NFL official is no easy matter: every week the NFL sets its officials written exams, at every game an NFL observer is present to check on their competence, and the officiating department in New York watches every game film every week and issues each official with a written report assessing his performance. During the regular season the officials are graded by the NFL, and only those with the top marks are allowed to officiate the play-offs, Super Bowl and Pro Bowl!

NFL Properties

NFL Properties is a vast organisation within the corporation — its primary job is to promote the image of the NFL and its teams, and it does the job with consummate skill.

NFL Properties own all the copyrights to the clubs' official logos and they control the use of these valuable commodities strictly. If a manufacturer wants to put, say, the Washington Redskins' logo on a jacket, he must first send a sample to NFL Properties. They then test the garment for quality and only if it passes their rigorous tests will a licence be granted — otherwise the NFL will refuse the application. Every item that carries a team logo and the NFL badge is a sign of good quality — there are over 350 officially licensed items ranging from umbrellas to sofas. This attention to quality control works wonders — in a recent survey 96 per cent of people questioned believed that the official NFL logo on an item meant they were buying something of the highest quality.

NFL Properties also publishes all official NFL books as well as the glossy *Game Day* magazine — the programme for every game.

The income from all of this is not just distributed to the club or kept in house. Since 1973 nearly a hundred needy organisations have benefited to the tune of over $6 million from NFL Charities.

NFL Films

Based in New Jersey, NFL Films are without peers in the making of sports-based films. Employing over a hundred staff, NFL Films has justifiably won major awards for its productions; and when the season starts the madness begins, as NFL Films records every game, processing and editing, sometimes overnight, to supply the world with top-class action.

NFL Public Service Programmes

The NFL sponsor public service adverts o. both radio and tv. These are adverts for organisations such as the American Cancer Society and the American Heart Organisation, featuring NFL players and coaches (and their wives), who give their time free; production is paid for by the NFL.

The NFL is of course delighted with the success of American football in Great Britain — the Commissioner Pete Rozelle told me he was as surprised as I was at how quickly the game had grown here.

It is interesting that when the British Football Association felt it was in dire straits, with the image of soccer at an all-time low, it contacted the National Football League to ask advice on how to improve the British game. It remains to be seen whether the British game will change, but it is inevitable that the NFL will continue to administer the American game with great skill, in the way only Americans know how.

Fair Play

If there is one word to describe the NFL's attitude to its 28 teams the word is 'parity'. The NFL through its extensive rule book does everything in its power to allow the weaker teams to have a better chance of improving from season to season, and through this formula the stronger teams are given a more difficult time.
The way this works is threefold.

Draft

The college draft enables a club to obtain new talent for its team from the cream of the nation's college players. There are two major scouting organisations, Blesto and United. The talent scouts from these two organisations trek round the country looking at and grading the college players, bearing in mind each club's different needs.

Obviously each team has its own scouts as well so by the time the draft comes along each coach has decided exactly what kind of players he needs. The method for deciding who gets first pick in the draft, i.e. the best player, is very complicated but in simple terms the club with the worst record gets first choice and the club with the best, the Super Bowl champions, goes last. This system is designed to balance the NFL teams. A lot of horse trading goes on between the teams who swop their choices around and it's the poor players who have to wait to see where they are going to be playing. 'It's the most difficult time in a player's life,' says Dan Marino, quarterback, with the Miami Dolphins, 'you sit by the phone not knowing when it's going to ring and when it does you are told where you'll be playing. It's a really tough time for a guy straight out of college.' This modern-day 'slave market' takes place in early May, and consists of 12 rounds lasting two days.

Once drafted by an NFL club a player cannot sign for any other club unless he is released, traded or waivered.

The waiver system is fairly elaborate but means that if a team places a player on 'waiver' the remaining 27 clubs 'file a claim to him' or pass the opportunity to acquire him. This 'I want him' 'I don't want him' business goes on during the off season for 10 days and again from early July until December. Eventually the clubs normally end up with the kind of players they want or will negotiate that the following year they will get exactly what they want.

The schedule

This is simple in theory, more difficult in practice. The theory is that the stronger teams from the previous season are allocated a tougher schedule than the weaker ones. So a Super Bowl winner will have to play the more powerful teams, thus making it more difficult for them to become champions again. The weaker teams have an easier ride as they are scheduled to play the less powerful and the weak can become strong.

Films/Video

Every NFL game is filmed by each club under very carefully laid down rules about angles of shots and editing. The film is then broken down into three separate needs — the offense, defense, and special teams. Why do the clubs have to film themselves? — it's not just so they can all admire their performance after the game.

The teams are required by the NFL to send their film — (normally within a day) to their following week's opponents. Now film which costs each club thousands of dollars a year is being replaced by cheaper and instantaneous videos.

Dick Butkus (Chicago Bears) certainly lived up to his nickname, 'the animal'. He was once charged with biting the referee.

Hardy (The Hatchet) Brown caused 21 men to be carried off the field in a single season.

★ HALL OF FAME ★

Every sport has its heroes, every sport has its stadiums — only American football has its saints and one central shrine. If American football were a recognised religion Canton, Ohio, would be its Mecca and the 'Hall of Famers' would be officially canonised saints.

The Pro Football Hall of Fame is a shrine to the greater-than-great of the game — nearly 4 million fans have paid homage since it first opened on 7 September 1963.

To be enshrined in the Hall of Fame is American football's greatest honour — more important than the Super Bowl, more important than breaking long-standing records, more important than Super Bowl touchdowns — to be in the Hall of Fame is the absolute pinnacle.

New members to the Hall of Fame, from all aspects of the game, are elected every year by a 29-member board of selectors comprised of media folk from every league city and the president of the Pro Football Writers' Association. Between 6 to 28 members are elected each year and to be enshrined a person needs at least an 80 per cent vote.

Any fan can nominate anyone eligible simply by writing to the Hall of Fame direct. Players must have been retired five years to be eligible, coaches who have just retired are eligible and owners and administrators can be elected at any time. The August 1986 induction of five new members brought the total number of members of the Hall of Fame to 133.

The Hall of Fame is in Canton, Ohio, 53 miles south of Cleveland, 100 miles west of Pittsburgh, 120 miles north west of Columbus and 225 miles from Detroit, Cincinnati and Buffalo.

Why Canton as the Hall of Fame site?

There are three very good reasons:
The American Professional Football Association, the forerunner of the NFL was founded there in 1920; the Canton Bulldogs were an early pro football powerhouse before the days of the NFL and the citizens of Canton organised themselves in the 1960s and formed a pressure group to persuade the NFL to put the Hall of Fame in their city.

The Hall of Fame is really something to see — if you are in the States it is well worth the trek to see all the exhibits. There are four separate buildings, a football action film theatre, a research library, a snack bar, a fascinating museum and of course the two 'enshrinement halls' where the greats of football are honoured for posterity.

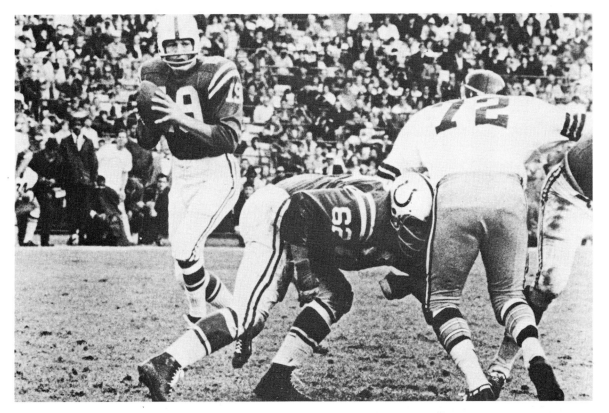

Above: **Johnny Unitas, a hero quarterback with the Baltimore Colts between 1956 and 1972, was enshrined in the Hall of Fame in 1979**

Right: **Sonny Jurgenson, a Hall of Fame member since 1983, who had an outstanding career with the Philadelphia Eagles and the Washington Redskins**

Every one of the current NFL 28 teams are featured in one exhibition area — and the Pro Football Photo Art Gallery features award-winning photos taken by some of the world's greatest photographers.

There is in yet another building, the 'adventure room' where through electronic magic the fans can actually participate in pro football history, and throughout there are taped recordings, question and answer panels and slide machines. Everything you ever wanted to know or see about pro football is there.

THE OWNER

Georgia Frontiere, owner of the Los Angeles Rams, is unique: she is the only woman in the NFL to run a team. Unlike other owners who take a back seat, Georgia (Gloria) is a very strong force within the Rams and is also extremely powerful in the male-dominated NFL.

She spends a great deal of time in London and has seen the growth of American football in Britain at first hand. It was she who initiated the idea of playing pre-season games in Britain.

Of all the team owners, she was the one I most particularly wanted to interview and I was delighted that she agreed to answer my questions, particularly as at the time of the interview the 1986 season training camp had begun. This is one of the busiest times of the year for an owner, assessing rookies and signing players.

Nicky Horne: What does an NFL owner do?

Gloria Frontiere: An owner sets the agenda for the whole team. He or she determines direction and charts the course the organisation will follow because he is responsible for all successes and failures. As in all businesses, an owner must be able to delegate . . . to allow managers to develop their potential. In these times a manager must also be of impeccable character. In some cases owners receive more recognition than most of the players, which is not necessarily a good thing, but it is certainly true.

NH: What is your day-to-day role?

GF: I try to talk with my department heads every day during the season about players' needs, concerns, injuries, acquisitions. What are the journalists writing and saying about us? In the off-season from January to July we devise plans to sell tickets and determine our sales strategies. We also do a lot of community relations work in the off-season.

NH: What is your relationship with Coach Robinson?

GF: I believe my hiring of Coach Robinson was one the most positive moves in my eight years. He is a great motivator who has led us into the play-offs for three straight years. The Rams are very fortunate to have John Robinson as coach. We have a very close working relationship. It is very important to give John everything he needs to create a winning environment. That includes the proper players and a positive attitude to the job. Things have worked out very well so far.

NH: You are the sole female owner in the NFL. What were the difficulties in the early years and how different is it now that you have a powerful voice?

GF: I'd like to think I have some influence among my NFL peers and would like to think I could continue as the only female owner in the league. I must admit I felt as though I was under a microscope in the early years. There was close scrutiny in the press and from other owners. They wanted to see exactly what the widow Rosenbloom knew about running a football team — could she do it? What they failed to understand was that this owner was anything but a rookie. I was with Carroll Rosenbloom for more than two decades and that time was a constant learning process. I felt that I was more qualified to lead than many of the newer owners. I made all the road trips with Carroll when he owned the Colts and later the Rams. I also knew the

Gloria Frontiere, owner of the Los Angeles Rams

game and what it took to build a successful franchise. That experience has served me well and served the Rams well.

NH: What are your earliest memories of American football? When were you aware of it in your family?

GF: I've always done very well in athletics. Sports were always important in my family as in most American homes. I knew pretty early on that I would be unable to play the game as a teenager and as an adult. But as a child I did pretty well, was one of the boys you might say. I could compete very well but it soon became obvious that I wouldn't be able to be on the team. Isn't it nice to own the team instead?

NH: How were you treated in the early days of ownership? How did you feel?

GF: There were times when I felt rather lonely. The press was writing negative articles, the criticism was intense. I sometimes wondered if the pounding would ever cease. I also wondered why they were doing this. There were teams with worse records and their owners weren't being castigated. Things have got better. Although every once in a while something will appear in a newspaper that I don't agree with that seems to be unfair. I've never asked for 100 per cent positive press. When we play poorly I can understand negative media reports. I just believe in a kind of consistency in the press. In a word, fairness.

NH: It was your idea to have a game in London. Why do you feel it is important?

GF: I do feel that it is important and have devoted nearly three years to helping to bring about an NFL presence in England. I would like to bring my team and other departments of my organisation to London to tour American military bases to let our servicemen know we appreciate their being there and that they have not been forgotten.

That was my plan last year. We fully intend to bring the Rams to England to all of the people, Americans and Europeans alike. We intend to do this because we believe it is important to our sport, our league and our country. We look forward to the day when the National Football League may be an international football league. A game for all people, not just American. The Rams want to do everything possible to make this dream a reality.

NH: What has been your experience of being a woman in male-dominated football?

GF: I believe I had to prove myself. I had to learn and learn quickly. Thank goodness for all my prior knowledge, otherwise the road would have been extremely hazardous. It hasn't been a walk in the park and I believe I have learned a great deal. I am fortunate to have an outstanding front office staff which I trust implicitly and that certainly helps me to do my job efficiently. I see myself as neither a feminist nor a crusader, but I hope my being where I am may someday help other women achieve the same kind of success and satisfaction I've had. What I've been doing is like climbing a mountain. I've had a few avalanches and I'm constantly being tugged as I move upward. There are those who would stop me from slowly making my way uphill to the top of the mountain. I can't look down but just keep looking up. I am constantly alert and aware that the unknown waits around the corner. But I know I can make it. I'm leading a lot of people who are counting on me to lead them to safety so I cannot and will not even think of failing them or myself. See you at the top!

John Riggins
Washington Redskins

John Riggins, the Man with the Golden Run, has no fewer than 11 club records to his credit. Inimitable, John topped the 1,000-yard mark for the fifth season in 1984 — making himself the oldest player at 35 in NFL history to gain 1,000 yards in a season. Beginning with the play-offs in 1982, he scored a tremendous 50 touchdowns in a 37-game span and his 84 points in 1984 tied for first position in NFC non-kickers. In 1984 he made the record game of his career with the Redskins.

Decidedly on the way up on that slippery ladder of the NFL record book, John is the number five leading ball-carrier with 10,675 yards, and third leading carrier. His combined yards make him the Redskins' all-time leading rusher with 6,795 yards on 1,812 carries. His NFL records include the most touchdowns in a season (24); the most rushing touchdowns in a season (24); the most consecutive games rushing for a touchdown (13) and the most seasons of 1,000 yards for a player over 30 years (3).

It's been, to date, an outstanding and esteemed pro career, well establishing his credentials for the Hall of Fame. Injury in 1977 put him on injured reserve, but with characteristic determination he earned the NEA Comeback Player of the Year Award in 1978 with a 1,000-yard season. A year later, in 1979, John made his best rushing game as a Redskin in the regular season with a 151-yard output in the season finale at Dallas — he broke a 66-yard touchdown run in the fourth quarter. Laid off in 1980, he sprang back into action in 1981 with a 126-yard effort in the win over Chicago while scoring two touchdowns. He went on to score his personal best with a three-touchdown game against St Louis.

Still on the way up the ladder, in 1982 John was named *Sport Magazine* most valuable player in the Super Bowl. A just reward for his outstanding play — 38-carry, 166-yard game. He was also awarded the Timmie Award from the Washington Touchdown Club. The following year the name John Riggins was to be seen everywhere: AP, UPI, *Pro Football Weekly*. Who could say enough about this outstanding player? He received the Bert Bell Award as NFL Player of the Year. It was undoubtedly a record-smashing year: NFL record 24 rushing touchdowns; a club record; career high 1,347 yards rushing. He lost the ball to the opposition just three times all year and that's not at all bad as he handled the ball some 468 times totalling up a string of 685 carries without a fumble. His play-off performances were quite simply scintillating — 119 yards against the Rams, and 123 yards in the NFC championship game versus the 49ers.

He left the Redskins in 1985, to retire to his farm. Football is less of a game without the 'Old Diesel'!

Todd Christensen
Los Angeles Raiders

Joining the Raiders in 1979, Todd Christensen has certainly proved his worth. By 1982, with 42 receptions for 510 yards, he became their leading receiver. The following year, 1983, he had a sensational 92-catch season; twice catching three touchdowns in one game — at Seattle and at San Diego. Undoubtedly a great year, he set the NFL record for catches by a tight end winning the league receiving title and taking the fourth position in NFL history (but has since been pushed back to fifth place). 1984 wasn't bad either, with a solid 80 receptions and receiving Pro Bowl honours for the second year running.

One of the old timers, but still a joy to watch. In 1986 Superglue Fingers caught everything that was thrown at him and finished the season as the NFL's leading catcher with a massive 95 receptions. It was enough to earn him yet another Pro Bowl place.

Phil Simms
New York Giants

'Blessed are the patient, for they shall be rewarded.' That beatitude could have been written for Phil Simms.

For eight years the Giants' quarterback sat at the sharp end of his team's mediocre performances, braving criticism and often abuse from success-hungry press and public.

As is often the case with pilloried sportsmen, his family also suffered under jibes that no Giants team would get anywhere while Simms was at the helm. But the relative veteran from Moorehead State weathered the storm to ultimately silence his critics on a sunny Southern Californian afternoon in January 1987. Simms was named MVP after a magnificent Super Bowl XXI triumph only a year after picking up the Pro Bowl MVP. He had repaid the faith which his coach, Bill Parcells, and the rest of the team had always placed in him.

Parcells said: 'Phil Simms was just unbelievable. He quarterbacked as good a game as has ever been played. This dispels for the last time the myth about Phil Simms.'

Before the game, Denver's John Elway had grabbed all the headlines. Superbowl XXI had never been billed as the clash of the quarterbacks and for many, Simms was an uncharismatic character, only there to make up the numbers.

While he was recognised as competent, the Giants' passing game was generally ignored. Simms went on to make a completion rating of 88 per cent, a new Super Bowl record, passing for 268 yards and three touchdowns. His 10 consecutive completions also made a new Super Bowl record.

The criticism rapidly turned to praise following his near faultless performance. Zeke Mowatt, who gratefully received a Simms pass to put his own name in the record books, summed up the mood of the celebrating Giants. 'I always told people that Phil was the one who could lead us to the Super Bowl. He really showed us his leadership today. We knew all week he was going to have a big game. It was only a matter of us running the patterns and getting open.'

Simms can now put the doubters behind him and establish himself as one of the greatest Giant quarterbacks of all time.

Todd Christensen

Walter Payton
Chicago Bears

Walter Payton, nicknamed 'sweetness', had a run of 12 successful seasons — not bad for the boy who didn't start playing football until he was 17. What's more, he's been collecting records and titles all the way. He owns the league single-game rushing record of 275 yards (against the Vikings in 1977) and heads the all-time rushing list. He's claimed 21 Bear records and six NFL records (rushing, combined yards, most 100-yard games, single game, rushing attempts) which includes taking an unprecedented five consecutive NFC rushing titles with 1,460 yards. At 23 he was the youngest player to be voted NFL most valuable player — that was in 1977 when his rushing total of 1,852 yards was the fifth highest total in NFL history. Not surprisingly, he also holds the Pro Bowl record for the most rushing attempts in a career.

In 1984 he was voted Black Athlete of the Year by black media members nationwide.

During the 1984 season Payton made his seventh Pro Bowl appearance. Surpassing Jim Brown he became the NFL's all-time leading rusher. He also broke both Brown's combined yardage mark and his record for most 100-yard career games. In 1985 he set an NFL record of nine consecutive games rushing for 100 yards or more. For years he *was* the Bears, breaking records when the team was mediocre. Since the Bears' rise to greatness from 1982 to 1986 the sky is the limit for this gifted athlete. When the Bears reached and won the Super Bowl in 1986 it was the crowning glory for Walter. Mike Ditka says of him, 'He's the best football player I've ever seen — period. At any position he's a complete player.' Walter Payton — an athletic genius.

Joe Theismann
Washington Redskins

Joe joined the Redskins in 1974 and in his rookie season with them hit 9–11 passes for 145 yards, returned 15 punts for 157 yards (10.5 average) and rushed three times for 12 yards and a touchdown. His first NFL start came in Week 5 of the 1976 campaign with a pass for 270 yards (20–37 and two touchdowns) and a run of 38 yards (one touchdown).

Made permanent starter in 1978, Joe passed for over 2,000 yards in each of seven seasons he has started. By 1981 he ranked in the top five NFC quarterback ratings in six categories: yards (third); completions (fourth); completion percentage (second); touchdowns (fifth, tie); lowest interception percentage (fourth, tie); overall rating (fifth). But that's not all — he also established a club record for pass completions (293) and was second all-time for season passing yards (3,568) and attempts (496). Joe was number one rated quarterback in the NFC in 1982 and made it to be a Pro Bowl starter. His great day came when he led the Redskins to a Super Bowl triumph completing 15 of 23 passes for 143 yards and two touchdowns. The accolades have certainly, and deservedly, poured in — in 1983 he earned the NFL title most valuable player award, Pro Bowl starter, named all-NFL by AP and the *Sporting News*, all-NFC by UPI, most valuable offensive player by *Pro Football Weekly*, Redskin player of the year by the Quarterback Club and offensive player of the year by the Kansas City 101 Club. Not surprising really, when you remember that during the season Joe completed 60.1% of his regular season passes, for 3,714 yards, 29 touchdowns and just 11 interceptions. What's more, his 417 yards against the Raiders was NFC best that year. He reeled off interception streaks and rounded off a truly memorable season by leading the NFC to victory in the Pro Bowl. His Super Bowl XVIII statistics — 16 of 35 for 243 yards.

Washington Redskins quarterback Joe Theismann became their 'record-player' in 1984 rising to the top of the team's all-time charts in attempts, completions and yards. He'd thrown for the three best games of his career: 17–20 against the Colts (85%); 19–24 against the Vikings (79.2%); and 26–33 against the Bills (78.8%). He finished among the top five NFC quarterbacks in five important categories: completions (283); touchdowns (24); yards (3391); interception percentage (2.7) and rating (86.6) The prowess of his running ability was shown off in full during 1984. Joe's 314 yards (on 62 carries) led all NFL quarterbacks. In addition he had individual runs of 27, 25 and 24 yards. So much for 1984, the year in which Redskin coach Joe Gibbs said 'Joe had a tremendous year for us in 1984. He had to adapt to all different receivers, two or three centres, and many blitzing defences. To go through all that and lead your team to a division title is something special: which describes Joe.' Praise indeed.

But that's not all – his average attempt of 8.45 yards is among the highest in play-off history. He left the Redskins in 1985 and began a new career with the CBS television network.

Dan Marino
Miami Dolphins

Never desperate, always dangerous — this young man is the best quarterback in the league today and has the makings of being the best of all time. Born on 15 September 1961 he displays one typical Virgo characteristic, the pursuit of perfection, and he comes very very close. In his second NFL season he was breaking records left right and centre, and finished the season as the NFL's leader in pass attempts (564), completions (362), yards (5,054) — 48 touchdown passes and an efficiency rating of 108.9 — you can't get much better than that. His great strength is his 'quick release' — he gets rid of the ball with such incredible speed and such deadly accuracy that defenses just can't get to him. He has an uncanny relationship with his wide receivers Mark Clapton and Mark Duper ('The Marx Brothers') and can throw long bombs to them with an accuracy that is the best in the league. His one fault is that he doesn't like to run with the ball. The reason is fear of injury — he has had several knee operations and this dislike of scrambling has denied Marino some chances. I remember sitting in the press box for one of the Dolphins' games when a player evolved where Marino could easily have run with the football — he didn't and was 'sacked'. I turned to my American football producer 'why didn't he run?' I cried.

'Marino is not paid to run' was the cynical reply.

Despite a mediocre season by the Dolphins in 1986, Marino finished only 0.1% behind the league's leading quarterback Tommy Kramer, with a percentage rating of 92.5. He was far and away the NFL's leading yardage gainer with 4,746 and notched up a massive 44 touchdowns, 19 ahead of his nearest rival, New York's Ken O'Brien.

Marino, who hails from Pittsburgh, splits his time between that city and Miami. In the summer of 1986, as he was about to become a father, I asked him whether fatherhood would affect him as it had done, say, John McEnroe.

'Sure, it will. I'm a family man at heart and I wanna spend more time at home, but it won't affect my game.'

'If it's a boy would you want him to follow in his father's footsteps?'

'Of course — no doubt about that.'

Well, when you're the best in the business that reply was what I imagined. If he stays healthy then the Hall of Fame is waiting for Daniel Constantine Marino Junior.

Jim McMahon
Chicago Bears

Quarterback Jim McMahon proved none too cuddly when he set three new Bear passing records in 1983: highest passing rating (78.5), highest completion percentage (58.4) and lowest percentage passes intercepted (3.96). His performances brought in the votes: UPI, NFC rookie of the year in 1982; PFWA, PFW *Football Digest* all-rookie; and the Brian Piccolo Award (1982). Injury plagued McMahon during the 1984 season. He suffered a hairline fracture to his throwing hand, severe back bruising and kidney laceration. Not surprisingly, he missed seven games and play-offs. In the 1985 season he really shone as the field general for the Super Bowl winning Bears. He is part of a great team but it was McMahon who put the Bears in the Super Bowl. His great strength is that he can control a game — if a play is sent in that he doesn't like he changes it. Against the Rams in the third quarter of the NFL championship game coach Mike Ditka sent in his own play, but McMahon disregarded it and got the game-winning touchdown. Rams coach John Robinson said of him after that game, 'McMahon was just outstanding today — he should get a lot more recognition.' McMahon has a healthy disregard for authority — he is the Johnny Rotten of the NFL, a punk who doesn't mind who he upsets from the commissioner down. He revels in being a bad boy and good luck to him!

Steve Largent
Seattle Seahawks

The seemingly unglamorous clash between the Seattle Seahawks and the San Diego Chargers in the early stages of the 1986 campaign brought together two of the greatest pass receivers in the history of the game, Charlie Joiner and Steve Largent.

By the end, both had rewritten the record books.

Largent's feat was to equal the record of Harold Carmichael with receptions in 127 straight regular season games. As the season progressed, he just went on extending his new record.

Steve's career has been a statistician's dream. Records have tumbled at almost every turn. He has completed nine seasons with at least 50 receptions, a record, and eight seasons with at least 1,000 yards receiving to go ahead of Lance Alworth.

He has had six seasons with 70 or more receptions and three (1978, 1981, 1985) with 1,200 or more yards.

And so it goes on.

1984 was a great year for Steve. He started all 16 games as wide receiver and led the Seahawks in receptions for the ninth consecutive season — earning his fourth trip to the Pro Bowl in the process. He finished fourth in the AFC and ninth in the NFL with 74 catches for 1,164 yards and 12 touchdowns.

He had the best day of his career against Denver, making 12 receptions for 191 yards with a touchdown, to take the game 27–24. Those 12 catches tied the team record, while the yardage well and truly topped the old marker of 173.

In the wild card game against the Raiders he was held without a reception for the first time in 110 regular season and play-off games. The Seahawks completed just four passes in 10 attempts. The following week in the match against Miami, Steve scored the Seahawks' only touchdown in the 31–10 divisional play-off. His six catches for 128 yards, including a 56-yard touchdown reception in the second quarter, were both Seahawk single game play-off records.

At the end of 1986, Largent talked of retirement, but it is likely he will be still there smashing records in 1987.

213

Marcus Allen
Los Angeles Raiders

The Raiders have plenty of reasons to be proud of running back Marcus Allen, the highest scoring non-kicker in the NFL. He topped the AFC running backs in receiving for three years, running 64 passes for 758 yards, and scored 44 touchdowns in 41 league games. In 1984 he rushed for over 100 yards three times, making a career total of seven. He missed starting just once in three seasons — playing in 41 games running and caught a pass in 27 consecutive league games. In 1983 he capped all his achievements by rushing 191 yards and taking two touchdowns (one a record 74-yard run) during the Super Bowl, earning himself the title most valuable player in Super Bowl.

Tom Flores the Raiders coach said when the Raiders acquired him 'Thank God for Marcus Allen'. Allen revitalised the Raiders with his speed and skill. Known as The Rocket Man because of his extraordinary leaping ability, Allen can sometimes play a little dirty but he delivers the goods consistently.

Joe Montana
San Francisco 49ers

There can be no doubt that Joe Montana's outstanding performance in 1984's Super Bowl XIX ensured his pre-eminence among professional football quarterbacks. With a magnificent 331 passing yards while completing 24 of 35 passes including three for touchdown, Joe set a Super Bowl record. Enough to bring great honours, but more than that, Joe brought to his team strong overall field generalship. Recognition was of the highest form — Super Bowl XIX most valuable player honours. But, great event though it certainly was, Super Bowl XIX was just one episode in the outstanding 'Joe Montana Story'. Its theme? — success, all the way! His talent, technique and temperament add up to victory. In 68 starts Joe's led the 49ers to the magical 49 victories (.721) and two Super Bowl championships. It is no surprise then to find Joe's name at the summit of the all-time NFL quarterbacks — his 92.7 rating is the best of any who've attempted at least 1,500 passes. In 1985 Joe, the NFL's all-time leading passer with a 92.4 career rating, finished third with 91.3.

Early in the 1986 campaign he suffered a back injury which required major surgery. Question marks hung over his career, doctors said he would not play again that season and maybe never again. Montana had other ideas and made a triumphant return a mere 55 days later. He went on to steer the 49ers into the play-offs, breaking team records along the way.

What makes him such a success? His scrambling ability, combined with his athletic powers of improvisation at the line of scrimmage. Quick feet, a quick mind, and one of the strongest arms in the game.

Marcus Allen

Tony Dorsett
Dallas Cowboys

Running back Tony Dorsett is the only NFL player to gain 1,000 yards in each of his first five seasons. With that kind of debut it's hardly surprising that he joined the very elite group of NFL performers who've rushed for 10,000 yards. In 1982 when he took his first NFC rushing title, he established an unbreakable NFL record by racing 99 yards from scrimmage to touchdown (Minnesota 1.3.83). For the Cowboys he's tops in rushing — eight in a row. He also claims the club's top five-season rushing performances, top eight single-game rushing efforts and the five longest runs from scrim-

mage (all 75 yards or longer). He took second place as the NFL's all-time leading play-off rusher with 1,325 yards in 16 games. And, of course, there are the honours. Apart from the undoubted honour of being team captain in 1981, 1982 and 1984, Dorsett was also voted to the Pro Bowl in 1978, 1981, 1982 and 1983. In addition, in 1981 he took All-Pro honours and was named NFC player of the year by UPI, the Washington Touchdown Club, and the Kansas City Committee of 101. And consensus rookie of the year honours were awarded to him for helping the Dallas Cowboys take the Super Bowl XII in 1978.

Football Techno-Speak

aerial game
A game where passes predominate.

audible
When a quarterback calls a new play at the line of scrimmage.

blitz
An attack from one or more linebacks or the defensive secondary against the quarterback. This is a tricky play because if the defense fails to blitz they have committed too many men, thus giving the offense a better chance.

bomb
A long pass.

clip
An illegal block from behind, normally directed at the back of your opponents' legs. Carries 15-yard penalty.

daylight
A hole in the formation of defense where a rusher can gain yardage.

dead
When the ball can no longer be advanced.

down
The period of action between a ball being put into play and going dead.

draw play
When the quarterback drops back as if he's going to pass but hands the ball to one of his backs.

flea flicker
This is a reverse (which is a play that begins in one direction and finishes in another), a lateral pass back to the quarterback who then throws a long hurl to a wide receiver.

fumble
To lose possession of the ball.

goal-line stand
Where the defense stops the offense scoring when they are a short distance from the goal line.

face masking
Grabbing another player's helmet — not allowed.

first down
When a team has gained the required ten yards in four downs, entitling them to another sequence of four downs.

hang time
The time the ball is aloft from when a kick or punt is taken.

interception
When the defense intercepts a pass intended for an offense receiver.

man to man
When the defensive secondary is responsible for a specific man rather than an area.

play action
A deceptive play by the offense to confuse the defense. It's normally faking running or passing.

pocket
The area of protection for the quarterback, behind the line of scrimmage.

punt
A long kick from scrimmage when a player drops the ball and kicks it before it touches the ground.

quarterback sneak
After the ball is snapped the quarterback runs or dives forward with the ball over the line of scrimmage.

roll out
Where the quarterback runs towards the side line instead of stepping back to throw.

rushing
Running with the ball on a play from scrimmage.

sack
When the defense tackles the quarterback before he's got the ball away.

screen pass
Here the defenders rush the quarterback. Two or more blockers move to one side while an offensive backfield player goes behind them to get a pass.

scrimmage, line of
The imaginary line between sidelines that separates the offense and defense at the beginning of play.

shotgun
Quarterback stands 6–8 yards behind the centre to give him more vital seconds to throw the football.

shut-out
A game in which one team scores no points

snap
The backward pass of the ball from the centre to a quarterback to begin play.

sudden death
Overtime play when the score is even at the end of regulation time. Pre-season and main season games have a maximum quarter-hour overtime period, play-offs and title games continue until one team scores and wins.

time-out
Interval when play is not going on and the official clock is stopped.

touchdown
When one team crosses the other's goal line with the ball — scores six points.

turnover
Losing the ball by a fumble or interception.

yardage
Distance lost or gained by the offensive team or a play from scrimmage.

It happened on 22 January 1984 while the Los Angeles Raiders were playing the Washington Redskins in Super Bowl XVIII. Almost 15 minutes into half-time in Salt Lake City the water main burst! The theory is that so many residents of the city went to the loo at the same time before the start of the second half that the increase in water pressure exploded the pipe.

Picture credits

All-Sport (UK) Ltd   pages 37, 47, 49, 50, 79 and 105

Bob and Sylvia Allen/NFL   page 181

Atlanta Falcons   pages 65 and 66

Vernon Biever/NFL   page 174

Buffalo Bills   pages 31, 68 and 93

Chicago Bears   pages 19, 20, 21, 71, 165, 207 and 211

Cincinnati Bengals   pages 71 and 72

Cleveland Browns   pages 34, 74, 76 and 77

Dallas Cowboys   page 216

Denver Broncos   pages 36, 81, 82, 83, 160, 162 and 170

Eastern Kentucky University   page 95

Eureka College   page 26

Green Bay Packers   pages 87 and 190

Harvard University   page 135

Houston Oilers   pages 44, 89 and 91

Houston Sports Association   page 97

Illustrated London News Picture Library   page 11

Los Angeles Raiders   pages 7, 30, 45, 98, 100, 205 and 215

Los Angeles Rams   pages 41, 103 and 201

Amos Love/NFL   page 182

Richard Mackson/NFL   page 187

Al Messerschmidt/NFL   pages 184 and 186

Miami Dolphins   page 209

Michigan, University of   page 163

Minnesota Vikings   pages 109 and 111

NFL   pages 174, 177, 179, 181, 182, 183, 184, 185, 186 and 187

New England Patriots   page 113

New Orleans Saints   pages 115 and 116

New York Giants   pages 35, 39, 117 and 170

New York Jets   page 121

Wayne Paulo   pages 52, 54 and 59

Pittsburgh Steelers   pages 127 and 128

PRM/NFL   page 183

Pro Football Hall of Fame   pages 16, 17, 23, 69, 108, 118, 131,151, 155, 157, 158, 173, 193, 195,199

Richard Raphael/NFL   page 177

Cheryll Roberts   pages 27, 57, 71 and 156

Rugby School   pages 12 and 13

Rutgers State University   page 171

San Diego Chargers   pages 138 and 139

San Francisco 49ers   pages 143, 145 and 146

Seattle Seahawks   pages 147 and 213

Tampa Bay Buccaneers   page 148

Washington Redskins   pages 150, 152 and 153

World of Sports Photos   page 55

Yale University   pages 14 and 24

Michael Zagaris/NFL   page 185